Ghana Our Nation

Pledge

I promise on my honour to be faithful and
loyal to Ghana my Motherland.
I pledge myself to the service of Ghana with
all my strength and with all my heart.
I promise to hold in high esteem our heritage
won for us through the blood and toil of our fathers.
And I pledge myself in all things to uphold
and defend the good name of Ghana.
So help me God.

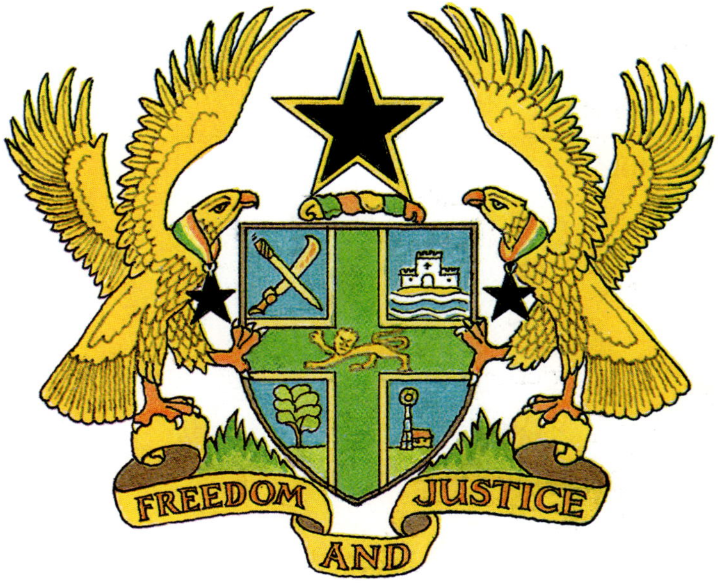

The National Anthem

God bless our homeland Ghana,
And make our nation great and strong,
Bold to defend for ever
The cause of Freedom and of Right;
Fill our hearts with true humility,
Make us cherish fearless honesty,
And help us to resist oppressors' rule
With all our will and might for evermore.

Hail to thy name, O Ghana,
To thee we make our solemn vow;
Steadfast to build together
A nation strong in Unity;
With our gift of mind and strength of arm,
Whether night or day, in mist or storm,
In ev'ry need what e'er the call may be,
To serve thee, Ghana, now and evermore.

Raise high the flag of Ghana,
And one with Africa advance;
Black Star of hope and honour
To all who thirst for Liberty;
Where the banner of Ghana freely flies,
May the way to freedom truly lie;
Arise, arise, O sons of Ghanaland,
And under God march on for evermore.

Pictures, Plans and Scale

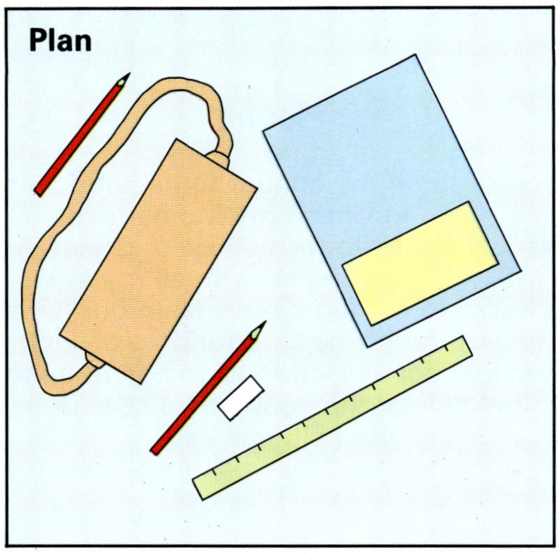

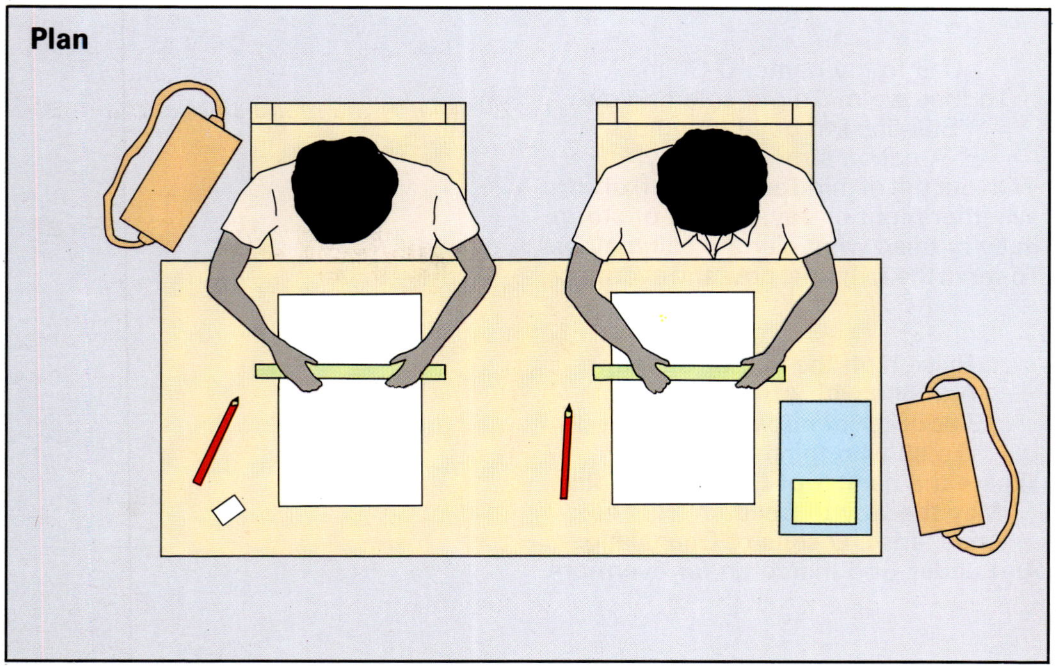

Pictures and Plans

Look at the left-hand **picture** of some classroom objects.

1. *How many different things can you see?*
2. *What are they?*

It is difficult to see what some of these objects are because they are hidden by other objects.

Now look at the **plan** opposite. This is what you would see if you stood on a chair and looked down from above. Now you can see the top of the objects.

1. *How many objects are really there?*
2. *Compare this to the number of objects you counted in the picture.*

Collect six objects and put them on the floor. Look down at them and draw their plans. Show your plans to a friend and let him guess what they are.

On the left is a picture of two children sitting at their desks. Their names are Ama and Kofi. They are measuring a piece of paper with a ruler.
Can you see the same objects that were drawn in the picture above?

Below is a plan of the same desk and chairs drawn as if you were looking down from above. Now you can see only the tops of the desk, chairs, books and rulers.

1. *Why are Ama's shoes not included on the plan?*
2. *Look at the shape of their desks and chairs. Draw the shape of your own desk and chair.*

Scale

This plan is much smaller than a **real** desk and chair. This is because it is drawn to **scale.** It is the same shape but much smaller in size.

To draw a plan of your own desk you need a **scale bar.** Your teacher will help you make one and show you how to use it. You will use a scale on which 1 centimetre on your plan represents 10 centimetres on your desk.
Using the scale bar and ruler measure the plan opposite and work out the real length of the desk.

1 centimetre on this plan represents
10 centimetres on the desk

Scale bar

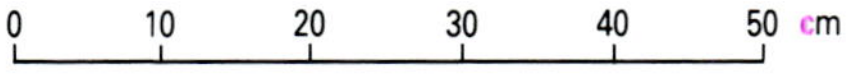

Classroom **Picture and Plan**

This is a picture of a classroom. Ama and Kofi are sitting together in the middle row facing the teacher. Look at the different objects in the picture. Now look for these on the plan below.

1. *Where is the blackboard?*
2. *How many desks are in the picture?*
3. *How many desks are in the plan?*
4. *Can you name something that is in the picture but not in the plan?*

Look at the plan of the classroom below. You can see all the classroom now. The children, teacher, books and pencils are not shown on this plan. The scale is too small to show each individual item. Look at the desks and chairs. They are set out in rows facing the teacher.
How are the desks and chairs set out in your classroom?

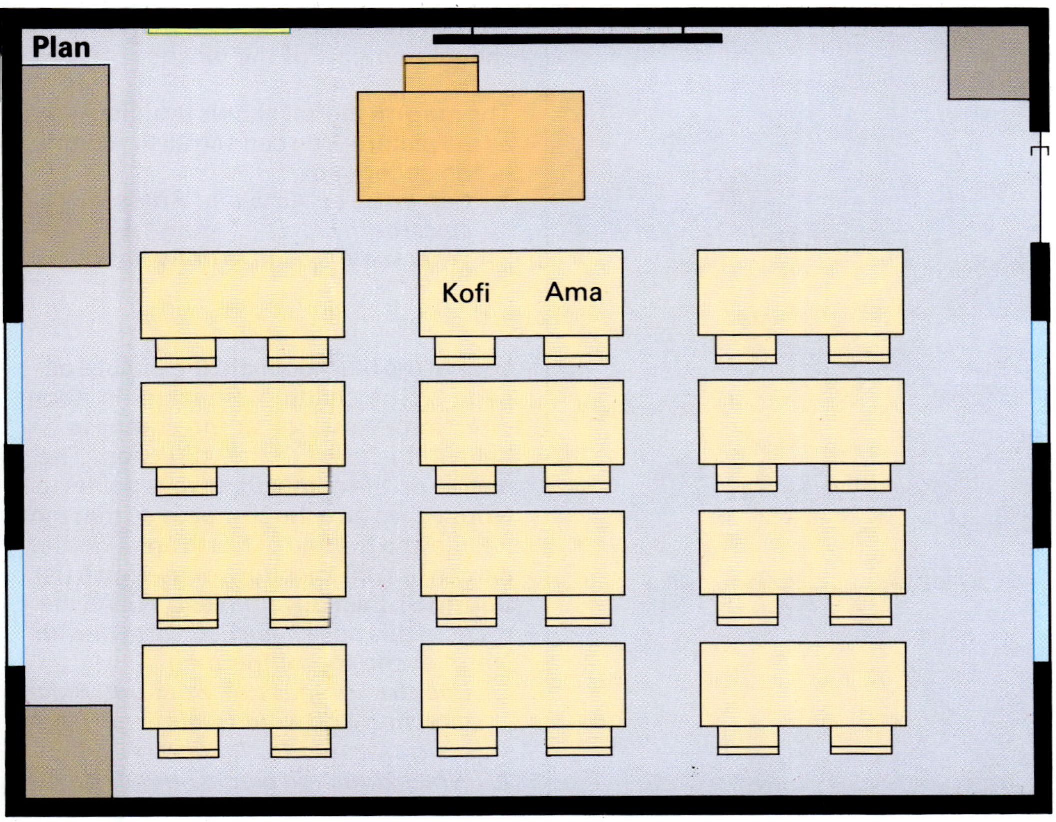

Key

Teacher's desk and chair
Children's desks and chairs
Cupboard
Floor
Blackboard
Wallmap
Window
Wall
Door

This plan has a **key**. The key helps us to understand the plan. It tells us the meaning of the different lines, colours, shapes and symbols used on the plan. Look at the key.

1. *What colour is used to show the teacher's desk?*
2. *What shape is used to show a window?*
3. *Work out how many cupboards there are in the plan by looking at the key.*

Look at the scale bar below. On this plan 1 centimetre now represents 50 centimetres. Trace the scale bar using thin paper. Now use this scale bar to work out the **real** distance on the plan.

1. *What is the real length of the teacher's desk?*
2. *What is the real distance from the blackboard to the back of the classroom?*
3. *Look at the picture again. Is it possible to work out real distances using the picture?*
4. *Now draw a plan of your own classroom using the same scale as this plan.*

1 centimetre on this plan represents
50 centimetres in the classroom

Scale bar

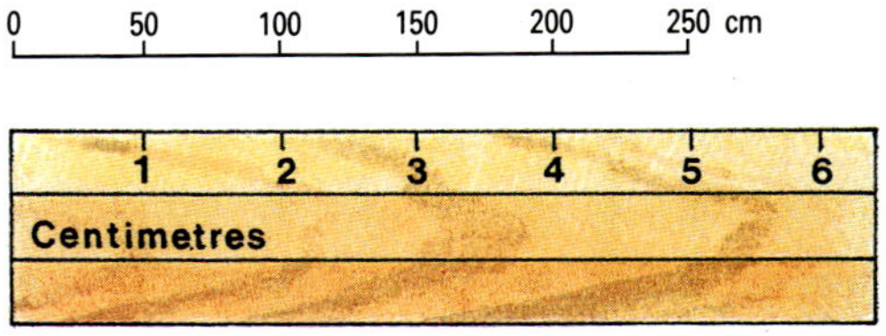

Picture and Map School and its Surroundings

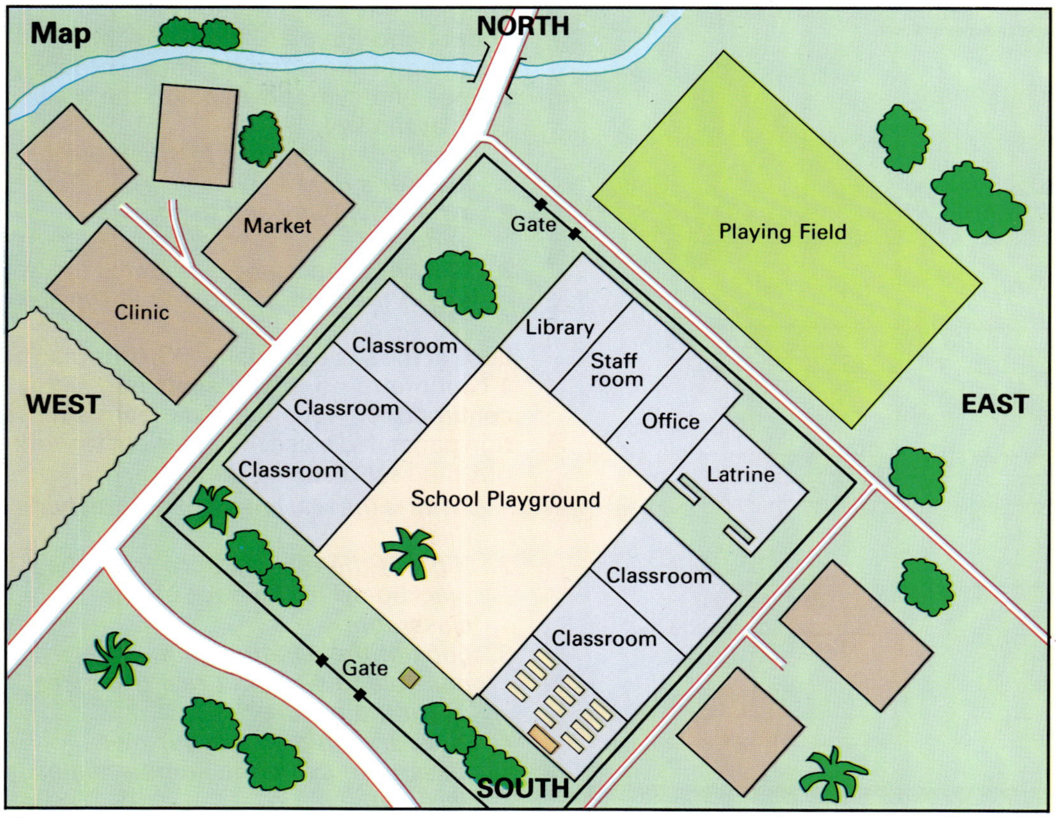

Look at the picture above. It shows the school and part of the village.

The **map** on the left shows the same area as the picture. You can see all the rooms in the school now.

1. *Can you see Ama and Kofi's classroom?*
2. *What scale is used to draw this map?*

Look at the blackboard in the picture on page 3. The children are learning about **direction.** Now look at the **compass** below. It is used to find direction. The needle on the compass always points to North. If we turn the compass so that the needle and the line of North are together we can find all the directions – **North (N)**, **South (S)**, **East (E)** and **West (W)**. All the maps in this atlas have been drawn with North at the top of the map.

1. *Use the compass to work out which direction Kofi would walk to get from his classroom to the library.*
2. *Which direction would he walk on his way back?*

Key

- School buildings
- Other buildings
- Field
- Open Space
- Trees
- Road
- Path
- Fence
- River
- Flagpole

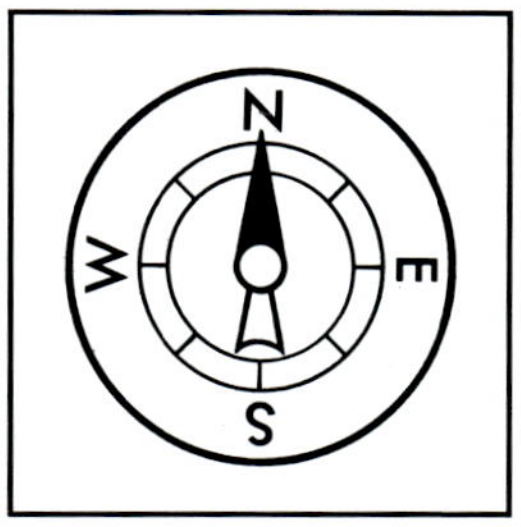

1 centimetre on this map represents 5 metres on the ground

Scale bar

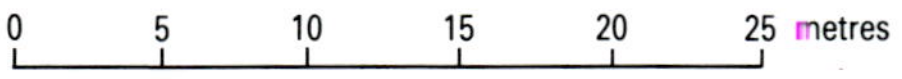

Village and its Surroundings **Picture and Map**

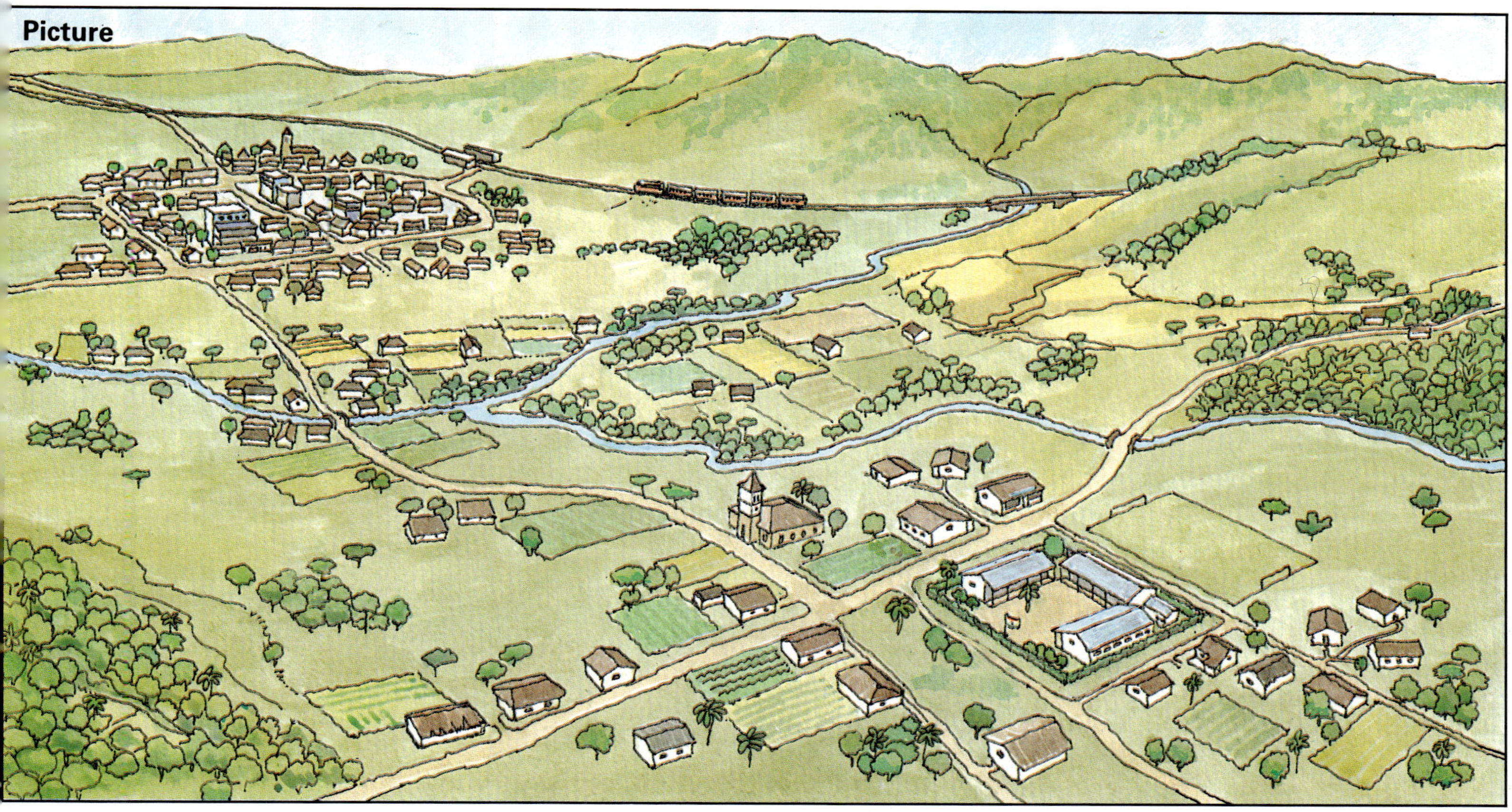

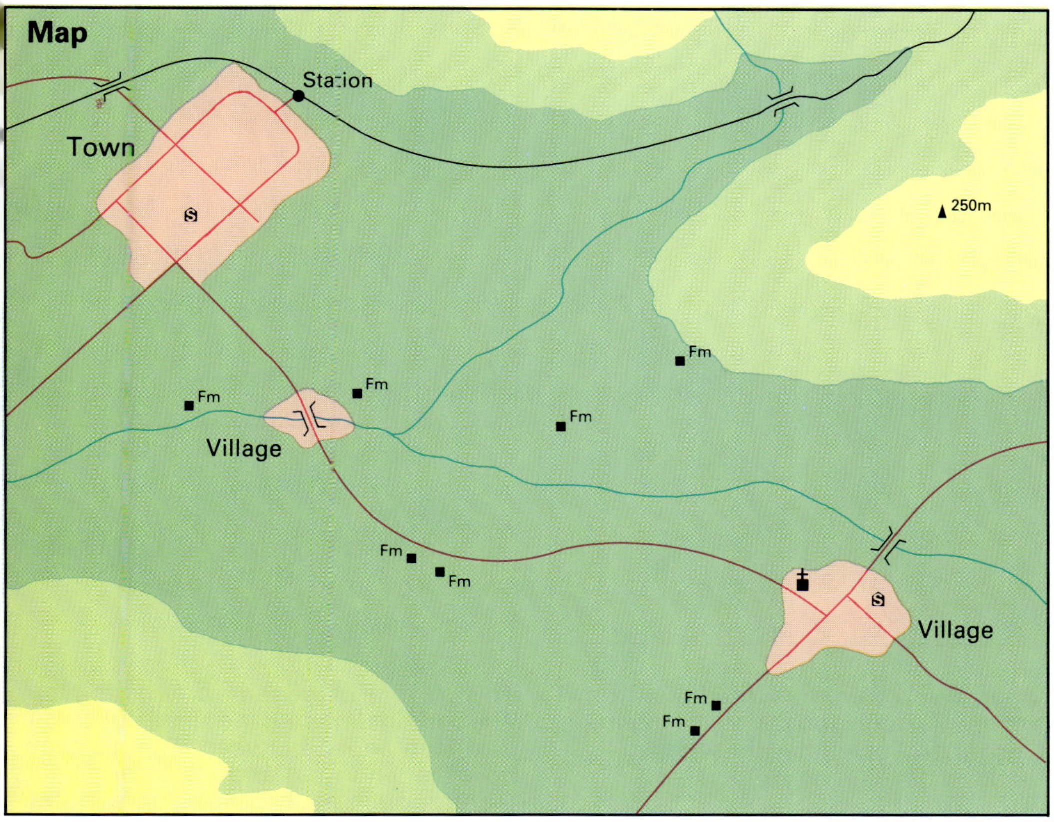

The picture above shows a much larger area than the picture on page 4. You can see the whole of the village and its surroundings.

1. *Can you still see the school?*
2. *What colour is the roof of the village church?*
3. *How many buildings are there in the village?*

On the left is a map of the same area as the picture. Compare this map to the one on page 4. You will see that less detail is shown at this scale. Only the most important buildings can be included. Look at the scale bar below.
What is the scale used on this map?

Now look at the key.

1. *What colour is used to show the built-up area?*
2. *Draw the symbol for a church and a school.*
3. *What colour and type of line is used to show the roads?*

Key

- Over 200 metres
- 100–200 metres
- 0–100 metres
- Buildings
- Road
- Railway
- Bridge
- River
- Spot height
- Church
- School
- Fm Farm buildings

1 centimetre on this map represents
100 centimetres on the ground

Scale bar

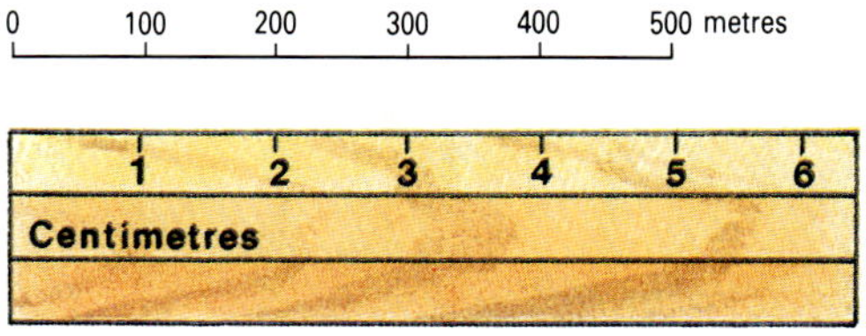

Ghana Pictorial Relief

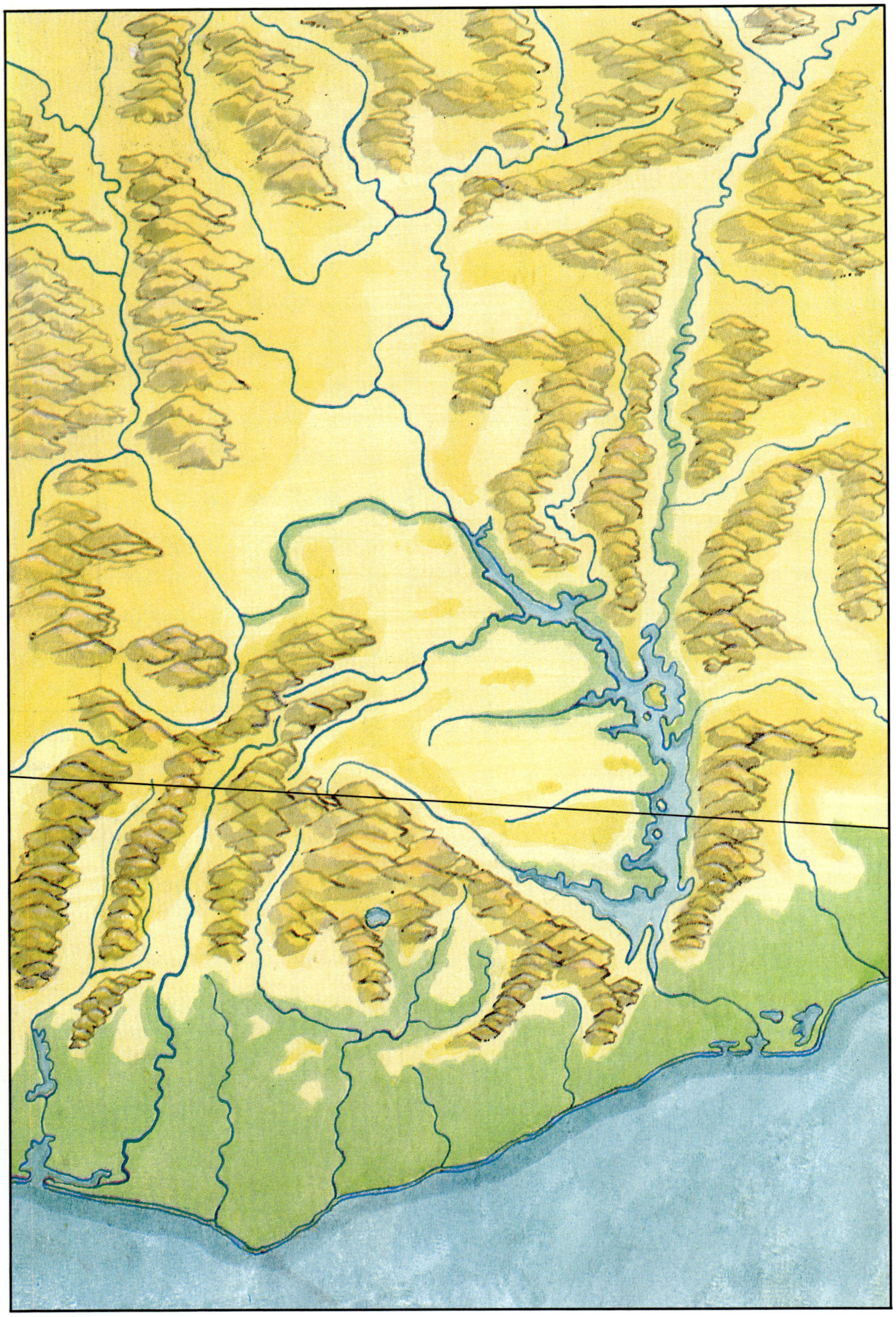

This shows part of the picture on the left, but added to it are lines joining places which are the same height above sea level. These are called **contour lines.**

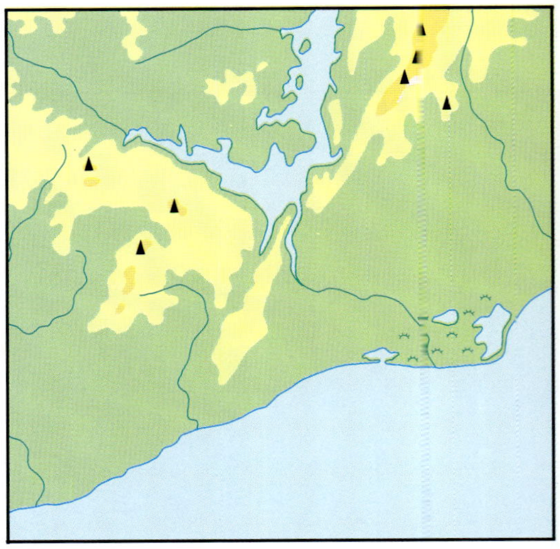

Key

Metres		
Over 500	▲	Mountain Peak
200 – 500		Marsh
0 – 200		

This is a **pictorial view** of our country, Ghana, as if you were looking down from space. It shows areas of hills and valleys, areas of low flat land and the river system. Many of the rivers flow into the large lake which then flows into the sea.

Do you know the name of this large lake?

Below is a **cross section** of the land taken along the black line on the picture above. Imagine you sliced the land in half along this line, this is what the cut edge would look like.

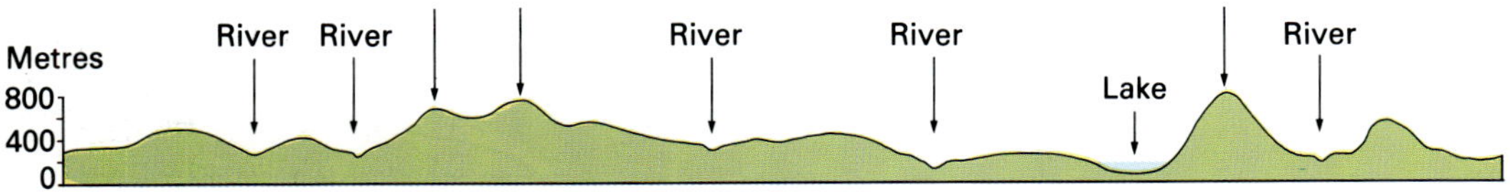

This is a **map** of the same area as above. The contour lines are the same but colour has been added between them to show how the land rises and falls. Certain features such as the mountain and the marsh have been shown with a symbol.

Under the map is a **Key.**

From this you can find out how high the land is in places and tells you what the symbols mean. Other types of symbol are often used to show the positions of oil wells, position of industries or airports, for example. See pages 16, 17 and 21.

Physical **Ghana**

Key

Metres

	Over 500	Mountain
	200–500	Upland
	0–200	Lowland
▲	Mountain Peak	

Dam
Marsh
International Boundary
Regional Boundary

0 50 100 150 kilometres

1. *What is the name and height of the highest mountain in Ghana?*

2. *Name the rivers which flow into Lake Volta.*

3. *Look at the map on pages 8–9 and name the regions which surround Lake Volta.*

Ghana Administrative

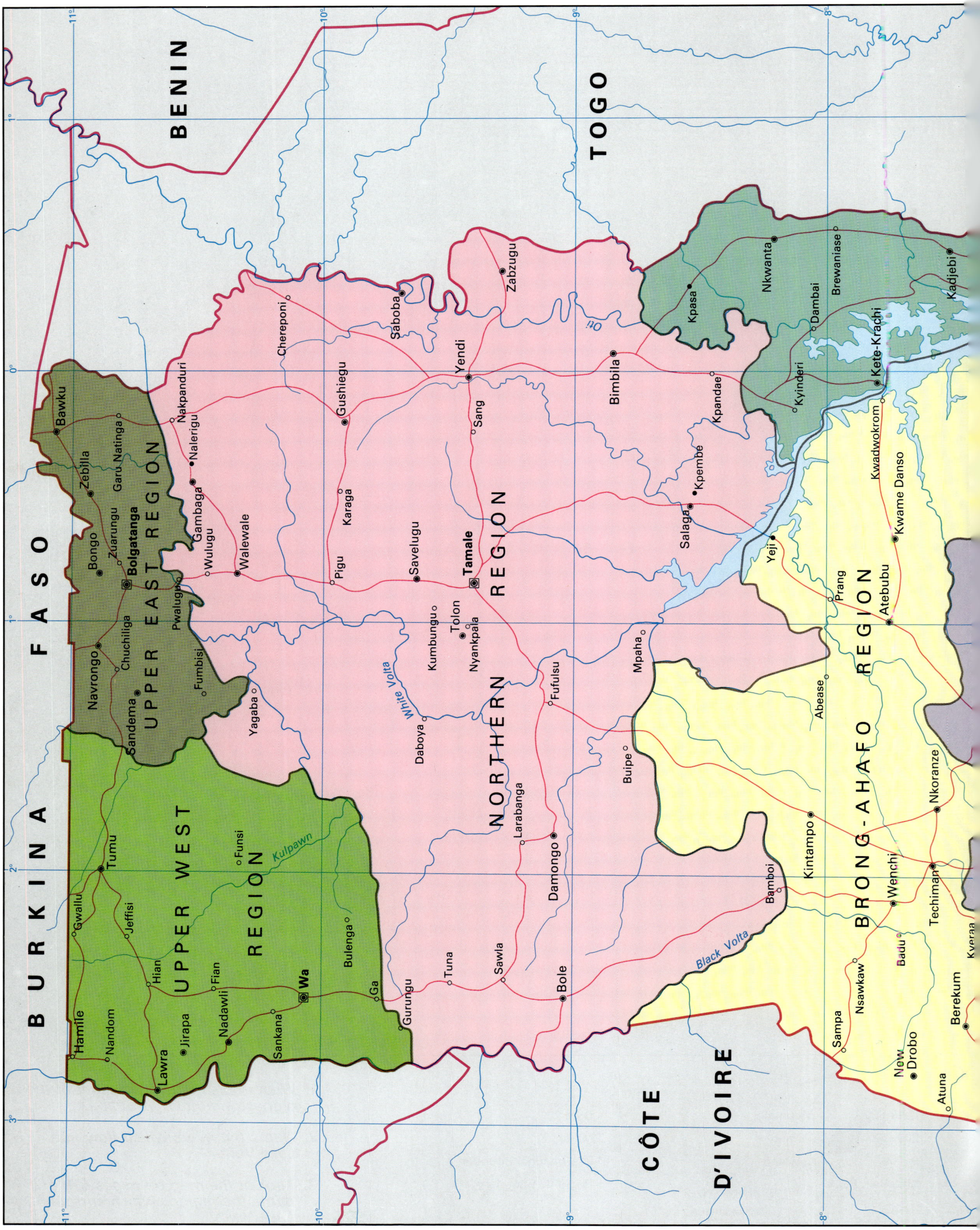

Key

(pink line)	International Boundary
(dark line)	Regional Boundary
(thin pink line)	Main Road
(thin black line)	Railway
▣	Capital City
◉	Regional Capital
●	District Capital
•	Important Town
○	Other Town

Scale: 0 20 40 60 80 100 km

Region	Area (sq. km.)	Population	Regional Capital
ASHANTI	24,389	2,762,400	Kumasi
BRONG-AHAFO	39,389	1,669,800	Sunyani
CENTRAL	9,826	1,423,000	Cape Coast
EASTERN	19,323	2,189,000	Koforidua
GREATER ACCRA	3,245	2,016,500	Accra
NORTHERN	70,384	1,649,200	Tamale
UPPER EAST	8,842	1,021,600	Bolgatanga
UPPER WEST	18,476	564,800	Wa
VOLTA	20,570	1,523,400	Ho
WESTERN	23,921	1,559,600	Sekondi

Parliament House, Accra the legislative branch of the government.

Ghana Rainfall

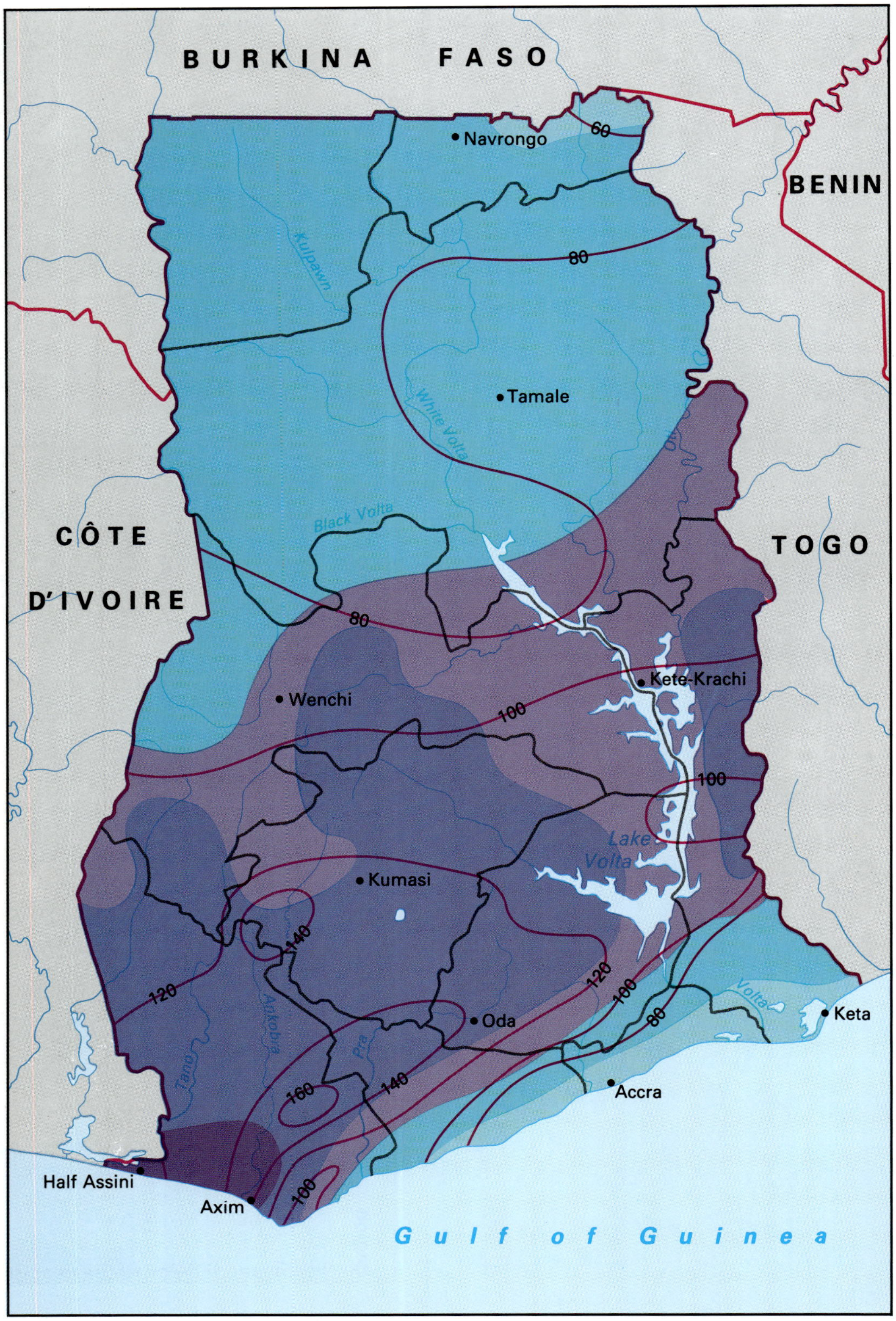

These are rainfall graphs which show how much rain falls during each month.

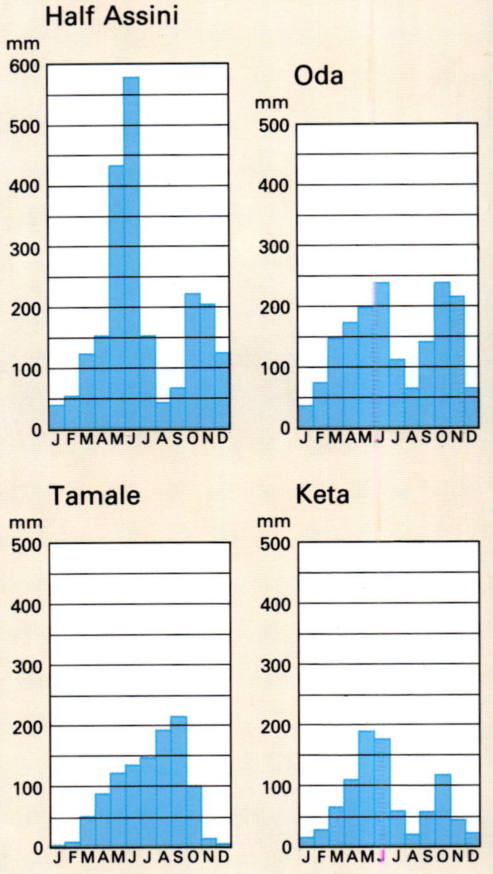

1. *Half Assini is a very wet place - during which months does most of the rain fall?*
2. *Keta is a very dry place - during which months does little rain fall?*

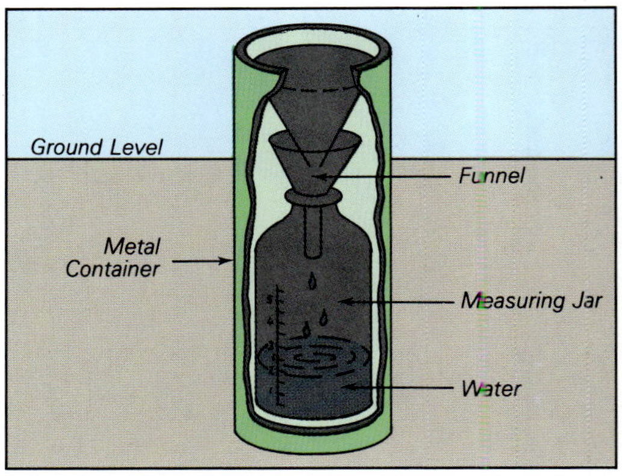

Key

Average Annual Rainfall
Millimetres

	Over 2000	Very Wet
	1500 – 2000	Wet
	1250 – 1500	Medium
	1000 – 1250	Dry
	Less than 1000	Very Dry

Rain Days

80 Average number of days on which it rains in a year

0 50 100 150 200 kilometres

1. Look at the map and write down
   a) which town has more than 140 days of rain in a year?
   b) which towns have less than 80 days of rain in a year?
2. Compare this map with the Vegetation map on page 12 and you will see that the rainfall and vegetation patterns in Ghana are very similar.
3. *What types of vegetation are found in areas with the most rainfall?*

This is a rain gauge.
It measures the amount of rain.
Make a rain gauge.

1. Put an empty jar in a hole in the ground.
2. Put a funnel into the jar as shown in the picture.
3. Measure the amount of water in the jar once every week.
4. Keep a record of how much water is in the jar.
5. Draw a bar graph similar to the ones on this page.

Seasonal Rainfall and Climate Charts **Ghana**

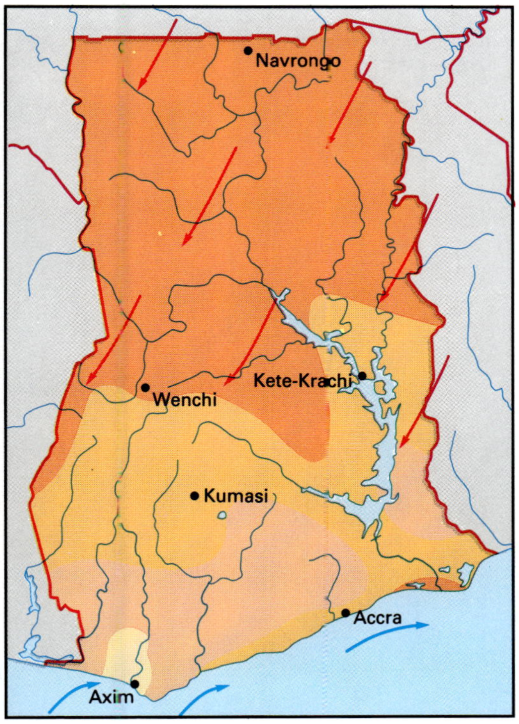

January – Dry Season (Dec. – Feb.)
From December to February the dry N.E. Trade Winds (Harmattan) are strongest. They originate from the Sahara and therefore do not carry any rain.

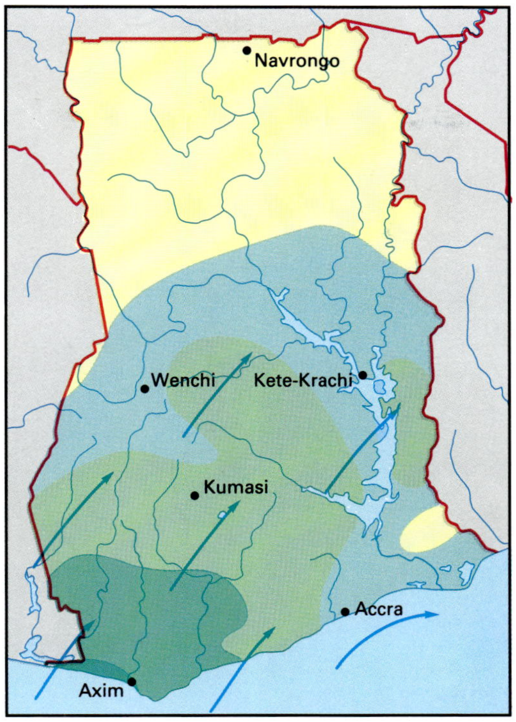

June – Wet Season (March – July)
The S.W. Winds (Monsoons) are strongest in the South West bringing much rain.

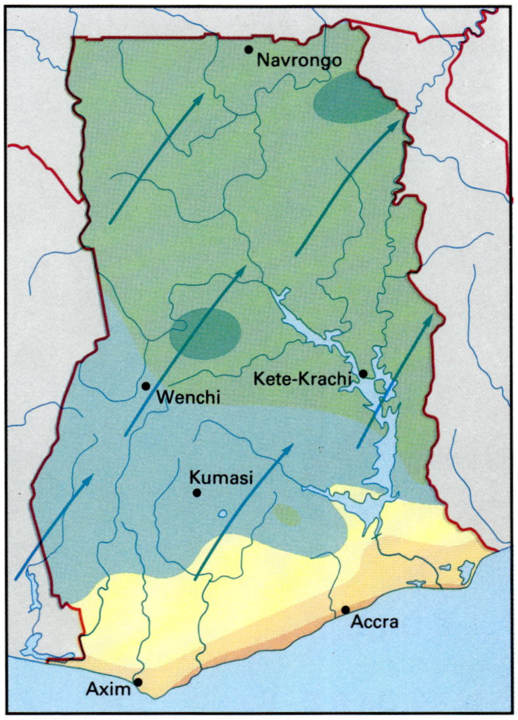

Sept. – Wet Season (Sept. – Nov.)
The S.W. Winds (Monsoons) are strongest in the north.

Most of the rain in Ghana is caused by the meeting of the moist S.W. Winds (Monsoons) with the dry N.E. Winds (Harmattan). The S.W. Winds are heated as they pass over the land. The N.E. Trade Winds cool the S.W. Winds and cause their moisture to fall as rain.

Key

Rainfall

Millimetres
- Over 500
- 250–500
- 200–250
- 150–200
- 100–150

Millimetres
- 50–100
- 25–50
- 10–25
- Less than 10

Winds

South West Winds (Monsoon) – cool and moist due to their passage across the Atlantic Ocean.

North East Trade Winds (Harmattan) – hot and dry due to their passage across the Sahara desert.

0 50 100 150 200 kilometres

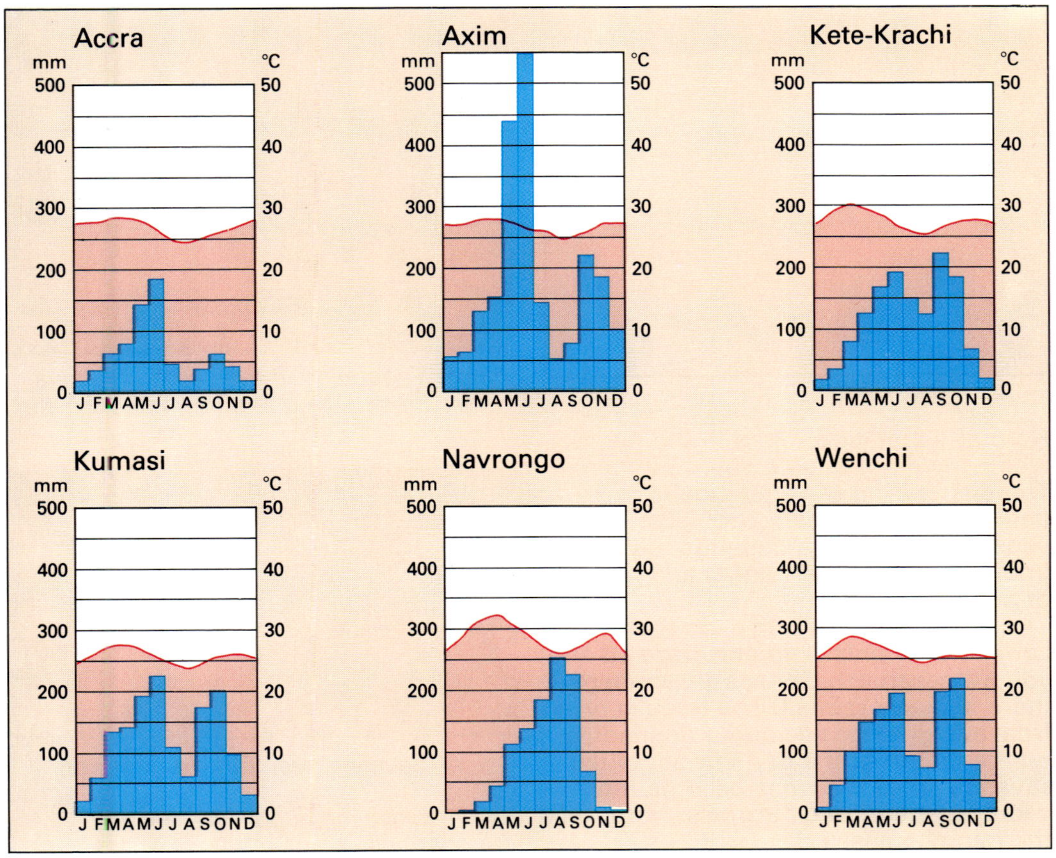

The main characteristics of Ghana's climate are
a) High temperatures throughout the year.
b) Large variation in the amount, duration and seasonal distribution of the rainfall from south to north.
c) Tendency for the dry seasons which separate the rainy seasons to grow longer and more intense with the distance from the sea.

The only significant division of the year in Ghana is into rainy seasons and dry seasons because the temperature varies little throughout the year.

Although the dry season enables recently cleared bush and the grass to dry before burning and it helps the cocoa beans to dry properly, it can do a great deal of harm to valuable crops if it lasts too long. Look at page 28 and you can find out why rainfall is so important for the growth of successful crops.

1. *Why does Axim have two distinct rainy seasons but Navrongo only has one?*
2. *At what time of the year are the harmattan winds strongest and from which direction do they blow?*
3. *Why does Accra have a much lower annual rainfall than Axim?*

Ghana Natural Vegetation and Soils

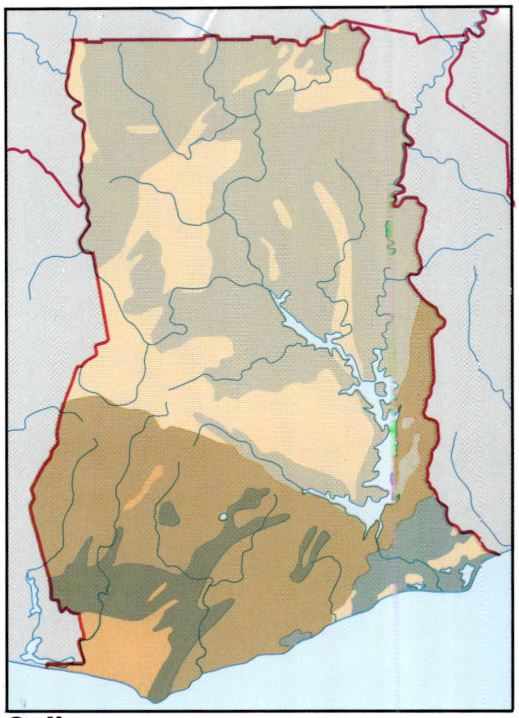

Soils

- Forest Ochrosols – well drained and fertile, most important agricultural region.
- Forest Oxysols – soils leached due to high rainfall, mainly tree crops.
- Forest Ochrosols and Oxysols – transition zone.
- Savanna Ochrosols – well drained porous loams which are extensively farmed.
- Groundwater Laterites – poorly drained loams provide poor livestock pasture.
- Coastal zone – variety of infertile soils, heavy clays which are waterlogged.

Soils are the joint products of rocks, climate and vegetation.

Jungle Vegetation in the south of Ghana, where there is high rainfall all through the year.

Key

Natural Vegetation

- Sudan Savanna – low grass with scattered acacia and baobab trees.
- Guinea Savanna Woodland – acacia baobab and shea trees with extensive high grass.
- Tropical Forest – moist mainly deciduous forest.
- Tropical Rain Forest – dense evergreen forest with a thick cover of undergrowth.
- Coastal Scrub and Grassland – dense scrub in the west and grassland in the east.
- Strand and Mangrove Swamp – patchy growth tolerant of salt water.

0 50 100 150 200 kilometres

Natural Vegetation refers to the plants which have not been planted by man. The distribution of vegetation is determined by climate and soils. The vegetation in Ghana depends mainly upon the amount of rainfall and length of the dry season.

Look at the rainfall map on page 10 and you will see that the forests grow where there is heavy rainfall. The trees vary from evergreen to deciduous depending on the length of the dry season. In the savanna lands the trees become more widely scattered and the grass shorter as the rain decreases.

Guinea Savanna near Tamale, northern Ghana.
Some cultivation is possible despite the poor soil.

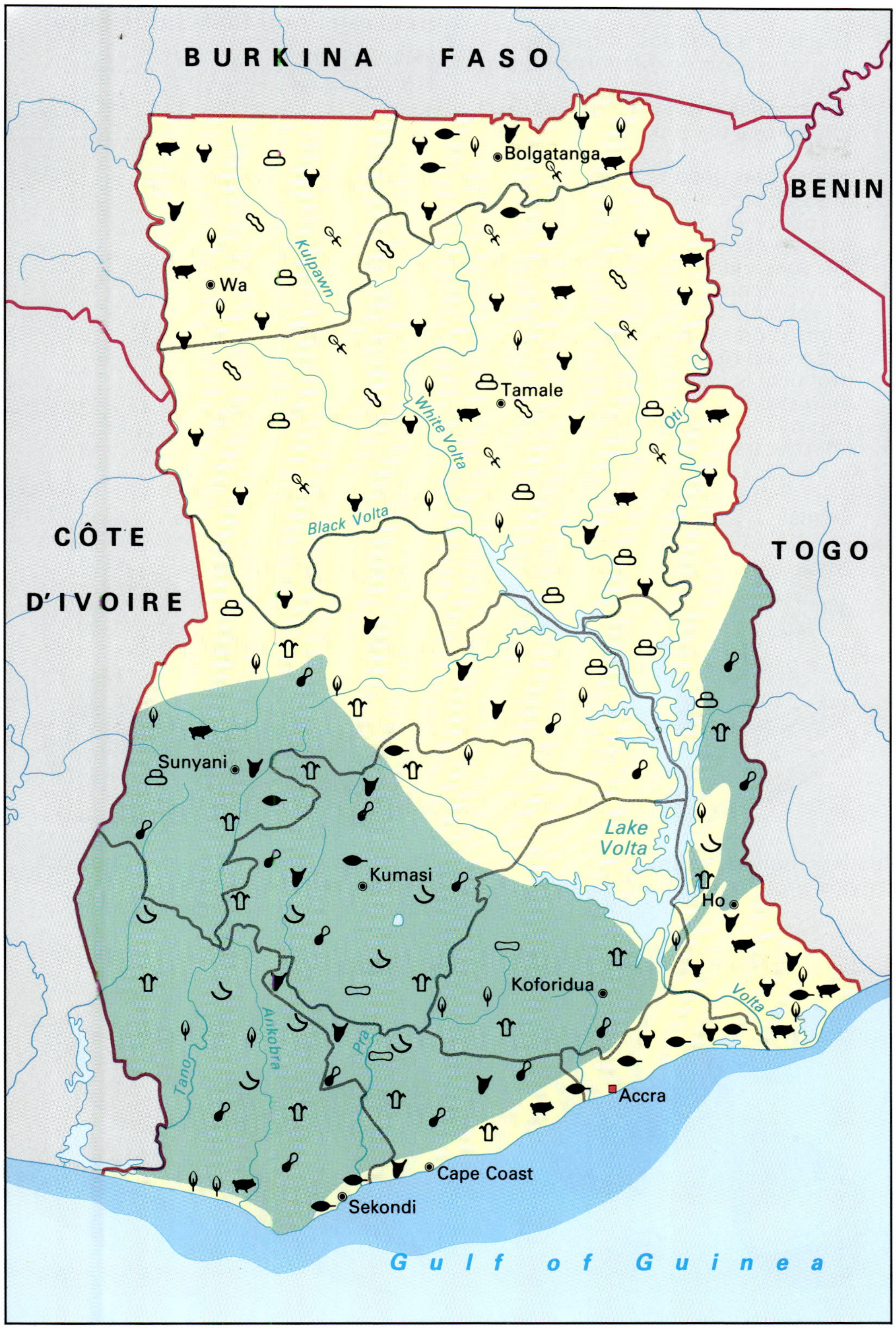

Key

Forest – root crop zone

Savanna – grain zone

Livestock and Fishing

- Cattle
- Pigs
- Sheep and Goats
- Fishing

Food Crops

- Cassava
- Cocoyams
- Groundnuts
- Maize
- Millet and Guinea Corn (Sorghum)
- Plantains
- Rice
- Vegetables
- Yams

0 50 100 150 200 kilometres

Groundnuts and Rice are also important cash crops.

Seine Net fishing is a traditional form of fishing practiced by the Ewe people. The nets are cast from canoes and then pulled in by large numbers of people on the beach.

A family harvesting their maize crop. Maize is the staple food crop of the majority of the people in Ghana.

Production of major food crops, 1996

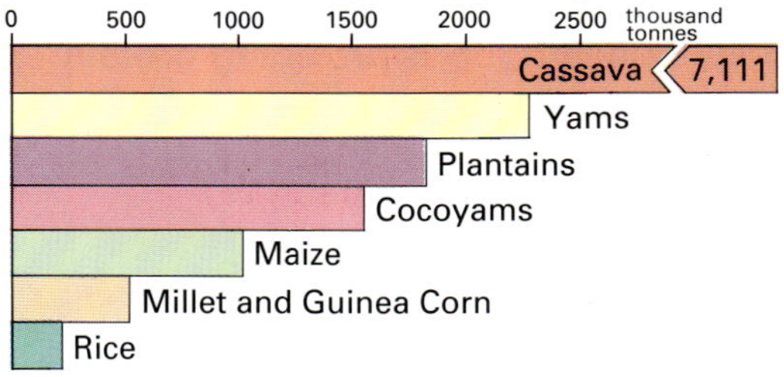

Ghana is primarily an agricultural country with nearly 50% of its working population in agriculture. Most farmers aim to feed their own families and produce some surplus for sale, these are subsistence farmers.

Ghana is not able to grow enough food to feed its population and has therefore become dependent on imported foodstuffs. Most of the food crops are grown by farmers with small holdings. These farmers do not have modern machinery, cannot afford to buy fertilizers to improve their land and often have problems transporting their produce to markets.

Look at page 14 and see how the government is trying to solve these problems and help Ghana become self sufficient in its food production.

1. *Which are the most important food and cash crops in your region?*
2. *Ghana caught 371,200 tonnes of fish in 1993, why is fish important?*
3. *Why are there no cattle raised in the forest zone?*

Ghana Feeding Ourselves

Ghana's Green Revolution

Ghana introduced a **Development Plan** in 1983 aimed at agricultural recovery and increasing the production of staple food crops especially cassava, maize and rice. This **'Green Revolution'** was launched to reduce Ghana's dependence on imported foodstuffs.

In the past Ghana has promoted cash crops but the problems of drought, an increasing population and a lack of funds has resulted in a shortage of Ghana's own food crop production.

Until recently there has been a lack of recognition of the critical role which the small farmer has in any **food self-sufficiency** scheme. 95% of the farming population in Ghana are small holders with an average farm size of 3 hectares. It is these farms that are benefitting from the new policies.

Aims

1. Teach new methods of farming.
   a) encourage crop rotation to benefit the soil.
   b) introduce chemicals and fertilizers to improve the productivity of the soil.
   c) use new seed brands.
2. Mechanisation – Labour saving tools.
3. Introduce methods of irrigating the land so that crops can be grown all the year round.
4. Provide incentives to farmers to make it profitable for them to grow food crops rather than cash crops. The price paid to the farmer for food products is very low despite rising market prices.
5. Improve storage facilities.
6. Improve transportation to the market.

Seeking Food Self-Sufficiency

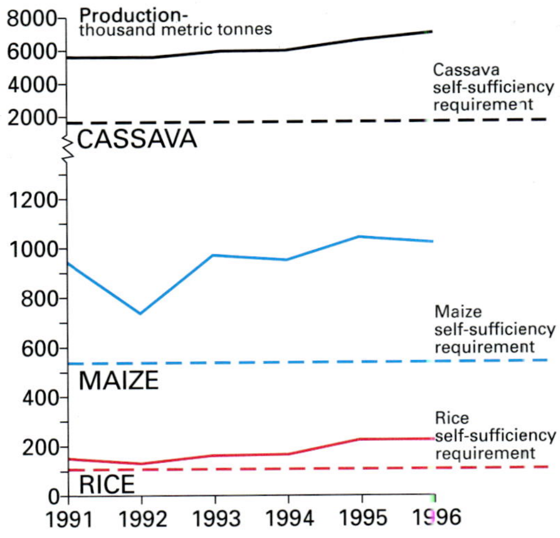

1. Animal Foods

Meat, fish, poultry, eggs, milk.
Body building foods providing protein and calcium.

2. Beans

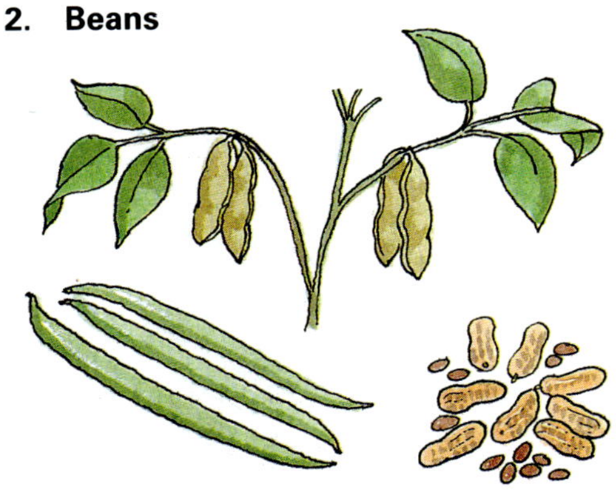

Beans, groundnuts, soya beans, peas.
Provide protein, iron and vitamins.

3. Fruit and Vegetables

Tomatoes, garden eggs, okra, spinach, cabbage, lettuce, carrots.
Important source of vitamins and calcium.

4. Grains

Rice, maize, millet, guinea corn.
Essential source of carbohydrates, iron and vitamins.

5. Fats and Oils

Palm oil, groundnut oil, coconut oil, shea butter.
Provide vitamins and give energy.

6. Roots

Yams, sweet potatoes, cocoyams, cassava.
Starchy foods, important source of carbohydrates giving energy and heat.

Good Food means Good Health

Substances obtained from foods are called **nutrients** which nourish the body. Foods supplying nutrients called minerals and vitamins protect the body against diseases.

1. Protein – body building foods.
2. Calcium – build strong bones and teeth.
3. Iron – help to make good blood.
4. Vitamins – prevent disease.
5. Carbohydrates – give energy and heat.
6. Fats and Oils – give energy.

Food Crop Calendar

for a farmer in southern Ghana showing some of the crops grown.

S Sowing
H Harvesting

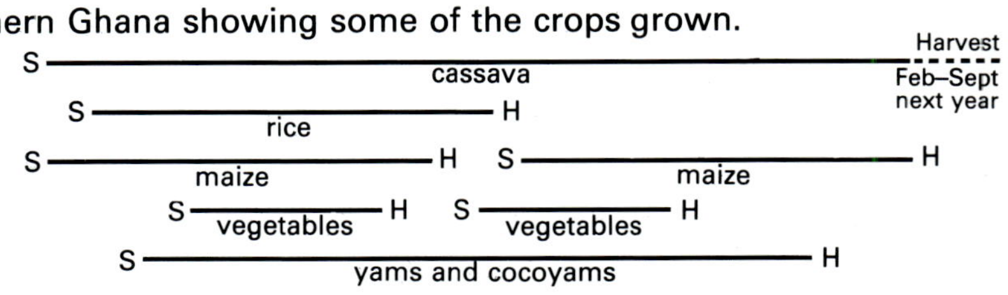

Prepare land			Sowing and plant growth				Harvest		Plant growth	Harvest	
Long dry season			Rain				Short dry season		Rain	Long dry season	
Jan.	Feb.	March	April	May	June	July	Aug.	Sept.	Oct.	Nov.	Dec.

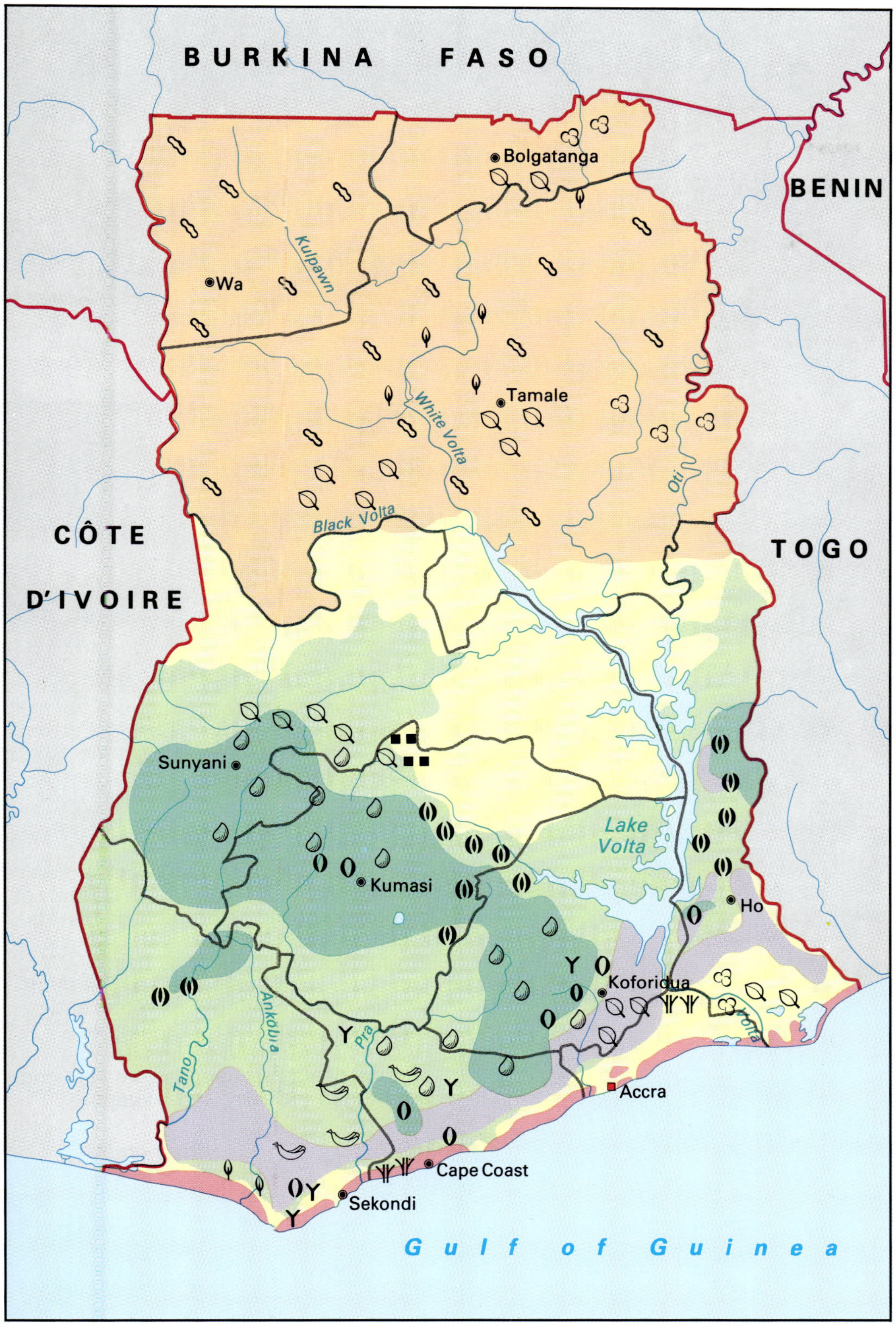

Key

- Cocoa – maximum production
- Limit of Cocoa production
- Coconuts
- Oil Palms
- Shea Nuts, Shea Butter
- Bananas
- Citrus Fruit (especially limes)
- Coffee
- Cotton
- Groundnuts
- Jute
- Kola Nuts
- Rice
- Rubber
- Sugar Cane
- Tobacco

Groundnuts and Rice are also important food crops.

0 50 100 150 200 kilometres

The oil palm is now increasingly used for the manufacture of soap. The kernel inside the nut is also processed to produce oil.

The cocoa pods are cut from the tree trunks and split open. The beans are covered to ferment and then laid on tables to dry.

Production of major cash crops, 1995*

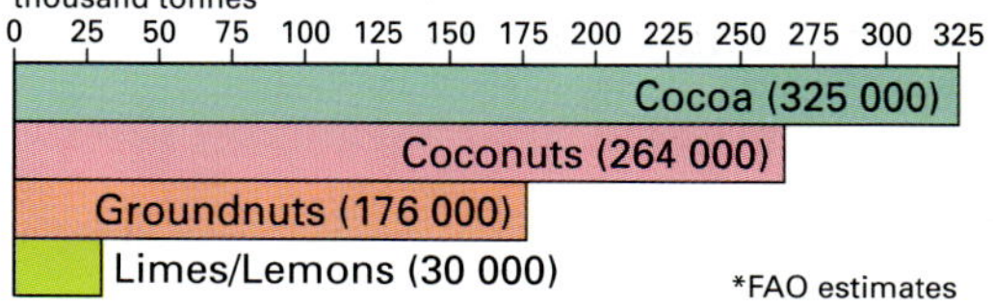

*FAO estimates

Other important cash crops include; bananas (4000 tonnes), coffee (3000 tonnes), palm oil (2500 tonnes) and tobacco (2000 tonnes).

The Importance of Cocoa

Cocoa is Ghana's most important commercial crop providing 27% of export earnings in 1995.

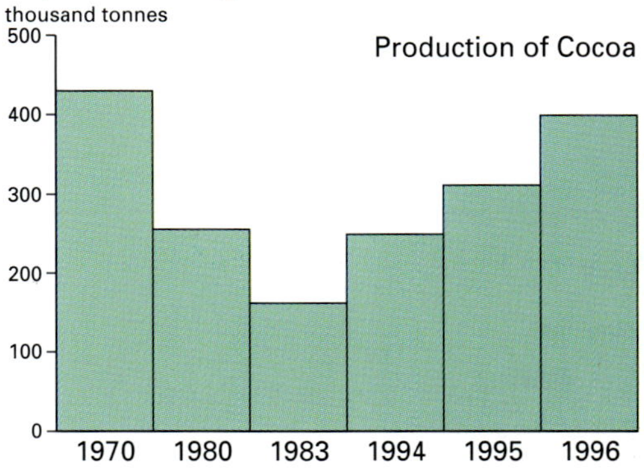

After the decline in cocoa production during the 1970s and 1980s the government launched a plan to redevelop the industry by giving cash incentives to replant the crop and importing new machinery and insecticides, and by introducing a new arrangement for paying the farmers, the 'Akuafo Cheque System'.

Ghana Minerals and Geology

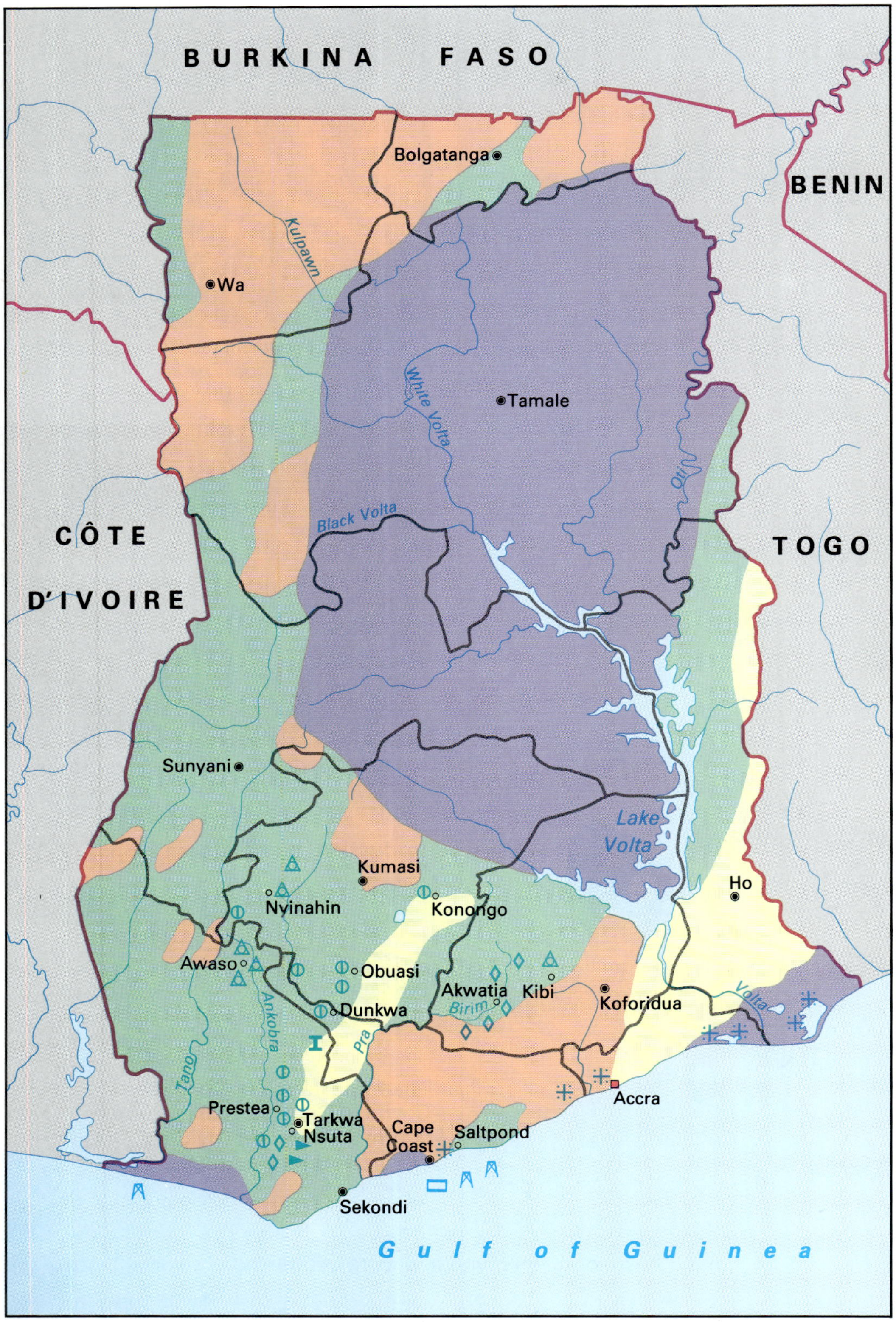

Key

Minerals

- Bauxite
- Diamonds
- Gas
- Gold
- Iron Ore
- Manganese
- Oil
- Salt

Geology

- Igneous Rocks
- Metamorphic Rocks
- Metamorphic and Igneous Rocks
- Sedimentary Rocks

0 50 100 150 200 kilometres

Minerals are found in the rocks beneath the soils. Unlike agricultural products minerals cannot be replaced when they have been dug out. Ghana has considerable wealth in minerals with vast deposits of bauxite still to be developed.

Gold mining requires a lot of heavy machinery. This shows the winding gear at the shaft head of the gold mine in Tarkwa, Western Region.

The manganese mine at Nsuta is one of the richest mines for high grade manganese ore in the world. The ore is used in the manufacture of steel.

The Mining Revival

Gold mining is the most important mining activity in Ghana, both in terms of employment and of the value of exports it generates.

Production of all minerals has been falling for many years due to the plant and equipment being in disrepair and to transport problems.

Ghana has received a considerable amount of aid to rehabilitate and expand the mining industry and transport network.

Gold
thousand ounces

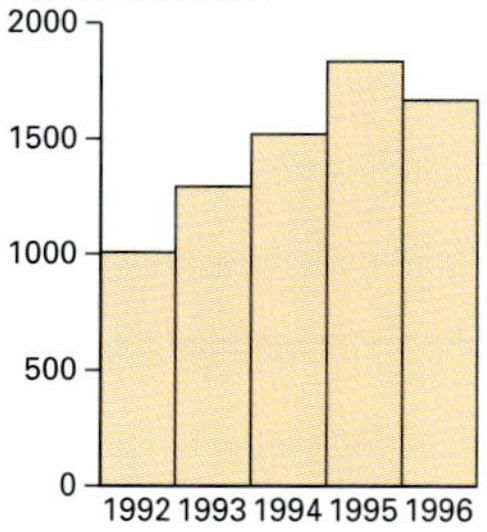

Diamonds
thousand carats

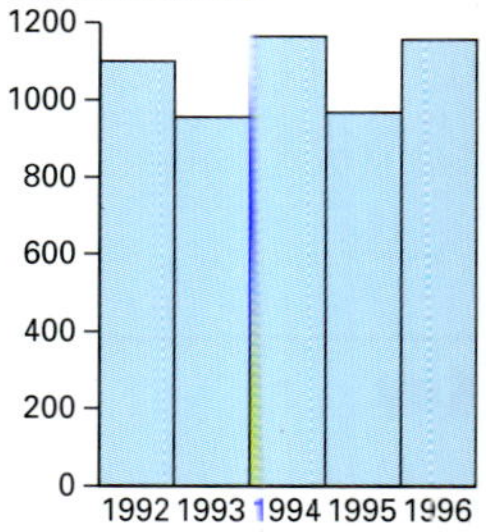

Manganese
thousand tonnes

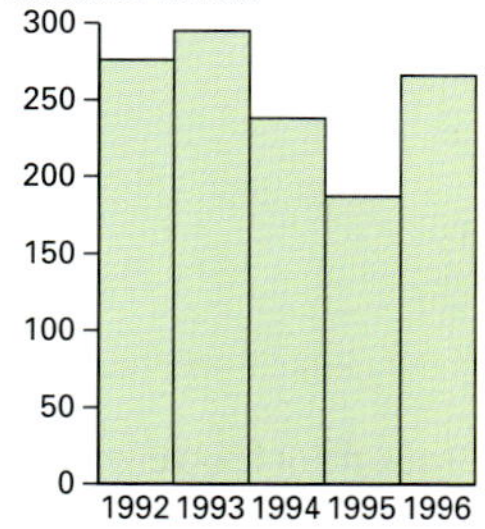

Bauxite
thousand tonnes

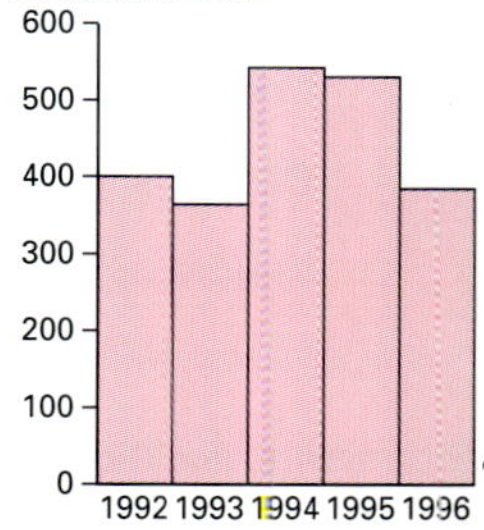

Why is Ghana's oil production important for the economy?

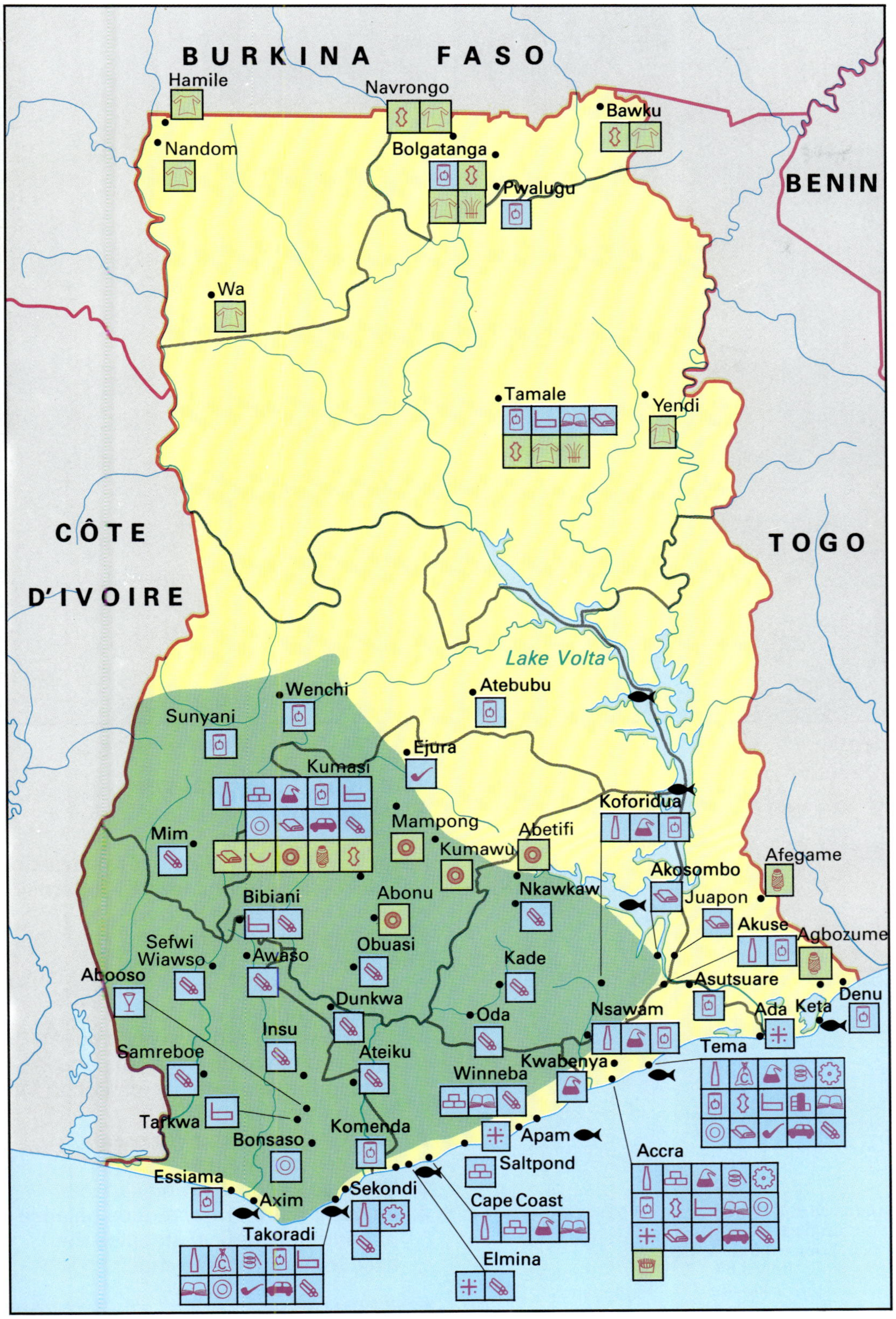

Key

Industries

- Beverages
- Building
- Cement
- Chemicals
- Electrical
- Engineering
- Food Processing
- Glass
- Metal Processing
- Oil Refinery
- Paper and Printing
- Rubber
- Salt Processing
- Textiles
- Tobacco
- Vehicle Assembly
- Wood Processing
- Fishing Industry
- Timber

Traditional Crafts

- Adinkra (Textile printing)
- Cane Products
- Carvings
- Goldsmithing
- Kente (Textile weaving)
- Leatherware
- Smocks
- Straw Products

0 50 100 150 200 kilometres

The oil refinery at Tema, Ghana's most important industrial centre. Oil is refined from the offshore Saltpond oilfield.

Log pond where the logs are debarked and treated before being exported or transported for further processing.

Factors affecting the location of industries

Industries are located according to which of the following needs has the strongest influence –

1. Raw materials
2. Power
3. Labour force
4. Transport
5. Market
6. Capital

For example Tema has developed as an important industrial centre because:

a) Tema is a port and a transport centre.
b) Raw materials and processed goods can be exported and imported easily.
c) Access to power from the Akosombo Dam.
d) Population centre providing labour for industry and a market for industry's products.

The most important group of industries is based on processing Ghana's own agricultural, forest and mining products.

Employment – % of the labour force employed in each sector.

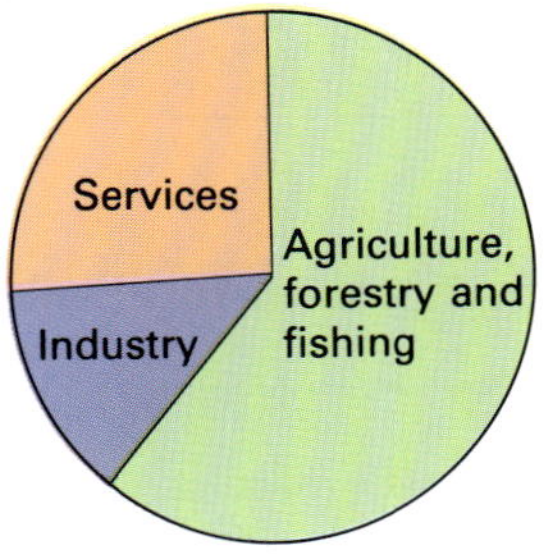

Ghana Trade

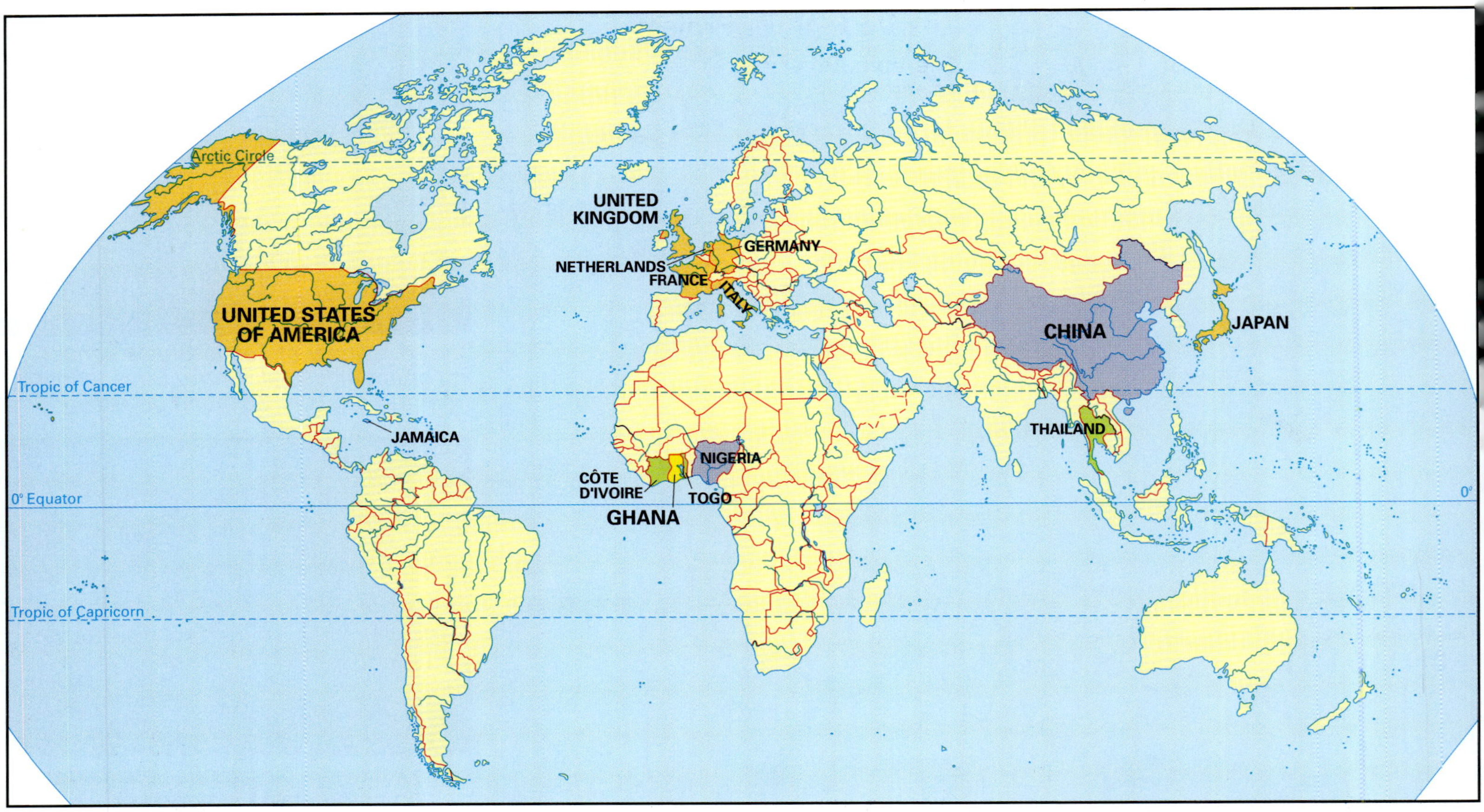

Ghana's Principal Trading Partners

Trade enables people, or countries to specialise in producing those goods they are most suited for, to sell their surplus to earn foreign currency and buy products which can be more economically produced elsewhere.

Key

Direction of Trade

- Major export market
- Major source of imports
- Country which is both a major export market and a major source of imports

Destination of Exports, 1995

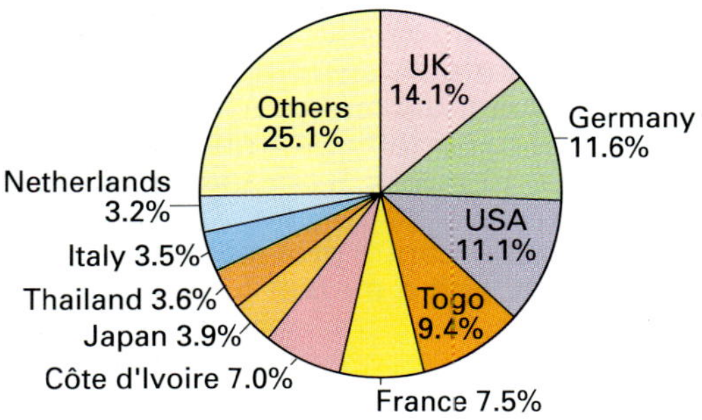

Source of Imports, 1995

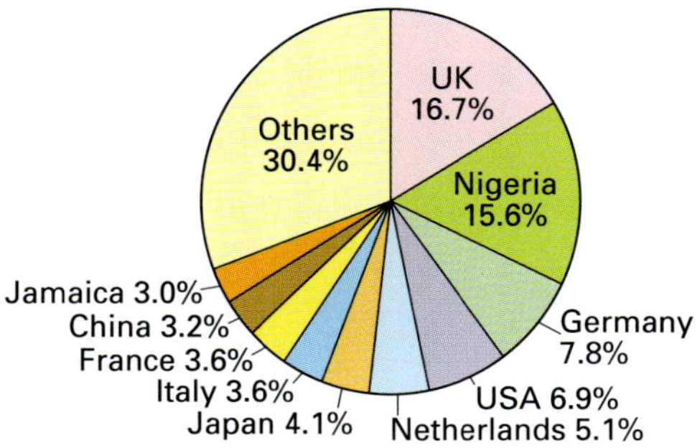

Principal Exports and Imports, 1995

Exports by % value. Total value US$ 1431.2 million

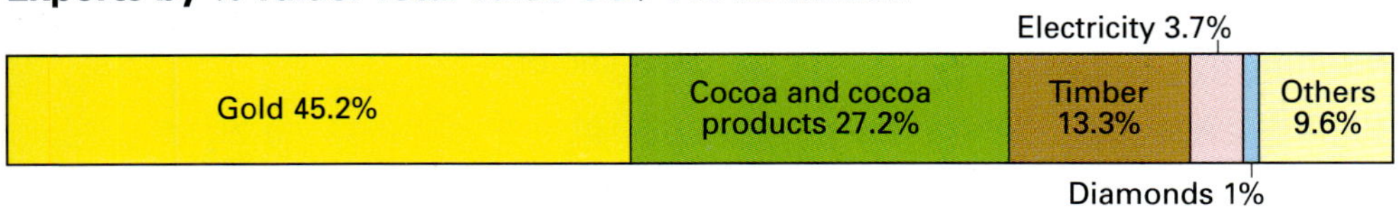

Imports by % value. Total value US$ 1687.8 million

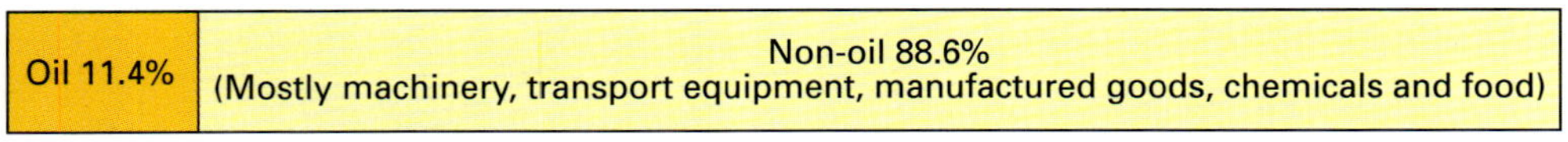

The Economic Recovery Programme

The government has launched a programme for economic reconstruction and development financed by external aid. This includes an **'Export Rehabilitation Programme'**.

The aims are:

1. Introduce incentives to increase agricultural and industrial productivity – move away from an import dependant economy and reduce the dependence on cocoa for foreign trade earnings.
2. Improve distribution of goods, services and income.
3. Improve export earning capacity.
4. Lower inflation rate; reduce balance of payments deficit; stabilise the exchange rate of the cedi.

The loading and unloading of ships at Takoradi port, Ghana's most important port until the opening of Tema port in 1961. Takoradi serves a large part of Ghana.

Akosombo Dam with Lake Volta in the background. In the rainy season the water level of the lake rises. The gates of the flood control dam have to be opened to stop water flowing over the top.

The hydro-electric power station at Akosombo. The electricity is transmitted, from the generators, by cables to the population and industrial centres of Southern Ghana.

How electricity is generated from water

A large quantity of water is needed to generate electricity. The water falls from the lake through six giant pipes into the power station below the dam. The vast quantity of water falling through the pipes gives the turbines in the power station a great push that starts them spinning. The turbines in turn drive the generators which produce electricity. Electric power generated from water is known as hydro electric power (HEP).

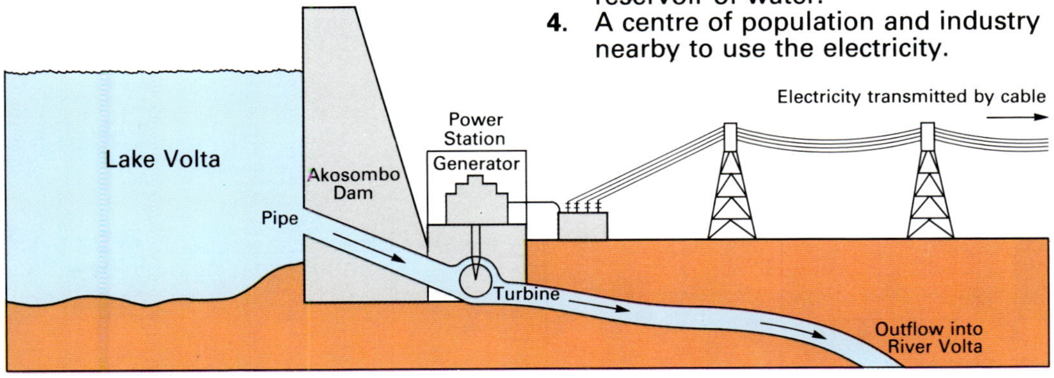

The Volta River Project

The Volta River Project was considered as early as 1915 but it was not until 1961 that the project was begun and it was completed five years later in 1966.

The dam across the River Volta was built primarily to create a vast body of water to be used for the generation of electricity. Lake Volta is the man-made lake which has formed behind the dam. The dam was built at Akosombo because this is where the river valley is at its narrowest.

The Akosombo plant supplies virtually all the country's electricity needs and also exports to Togo and Benin.

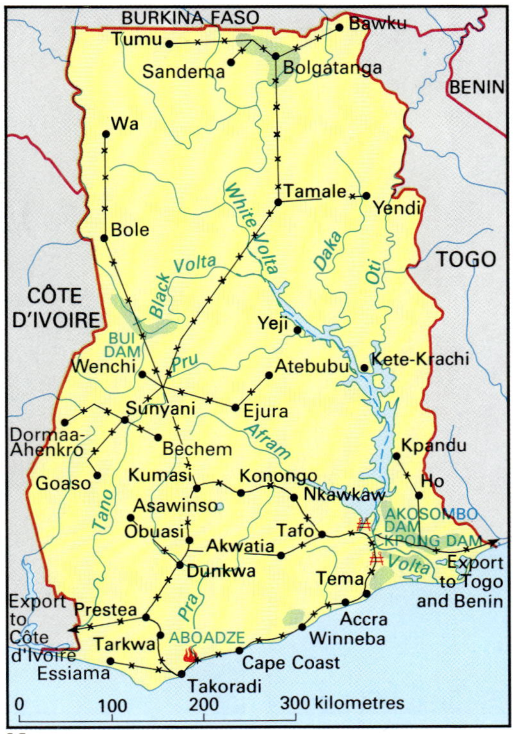

Key

- Important irrigation projects
- Course of the river Volta before the dam was constructed
- Power lines
- Hydro-electric power station
- Thermal power station
- Dam

Requirements of an HEP station

1. A constant supply of fast flowing water.
2. A valley suitable for building a dam.
3. Non-porous rock beneath the reservoir of water.
4. A centre of population and industry nearby to use the electricity.

The permanent irrigation of the dry south-eastern plains, using water from Lake Volta, has resulted in a substantial increase in productivity of cash crops such as sugar cane, rice, fruit and vegetables.

Uses

The Volta River Project is a multi purpose project because its uses are varied–

1. The generation of electricity for
   a) Domestic use in homes throughout southern Ghana
   b) Industrial use in new factories especially in the major industrial centre at Tema. The VALCO aluminium smelter uses 60% of the dams electricity supply.
   c) Export to the neighbouring countries, Benin and Togo.
2. Lake Volta provides a good north-south transport route for both cargo and passengers. Lake cargoes include agricultural products, fish charcoal, firewood, cement and household goods.
3. An important fishing industry has been developed. The lake was stocked with fish providing employment and a valuable source of food protein.
4. The lake provides a source of water for irrigating crops on the dry south-eastern plains and water pipes provide drinking water for cattle and the irrigation of pastures. As the water level in the lake falls during the dry season a wide variety of food crops can be grown on the moist exposed soils.

Advantages of HEP

1. It is cheap to run because the water does not have to be dug out of the ground or imported.
2. The fuel source, running water cannot be exhausted unlike oil and coal.
3. It causes little pollution.
4. The lake can be used for fishing, transport and providing water for irrigation.

1. *The Volta River Project is the most important project - are there any other river projects in Ghana?*
2. *Which mining centres and industries use electricity from Akosombo?*

Ghana Population, Ethnic Groups and Languages

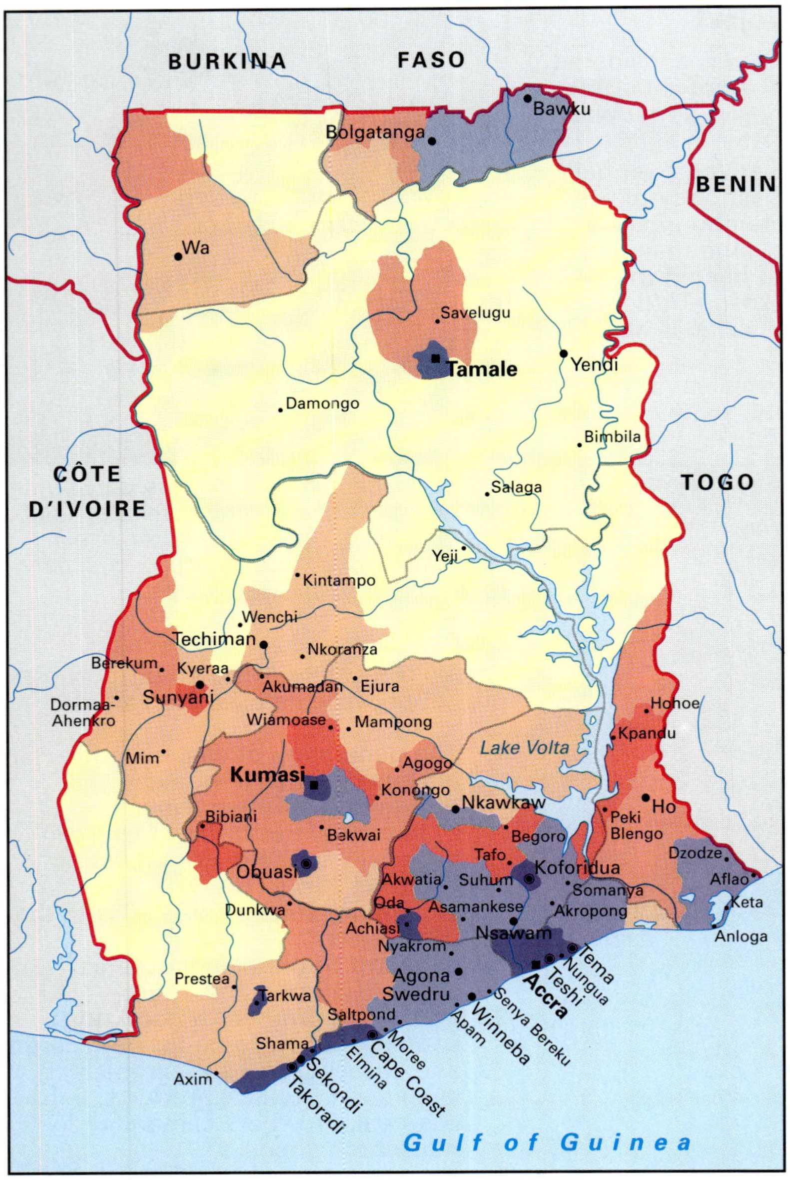

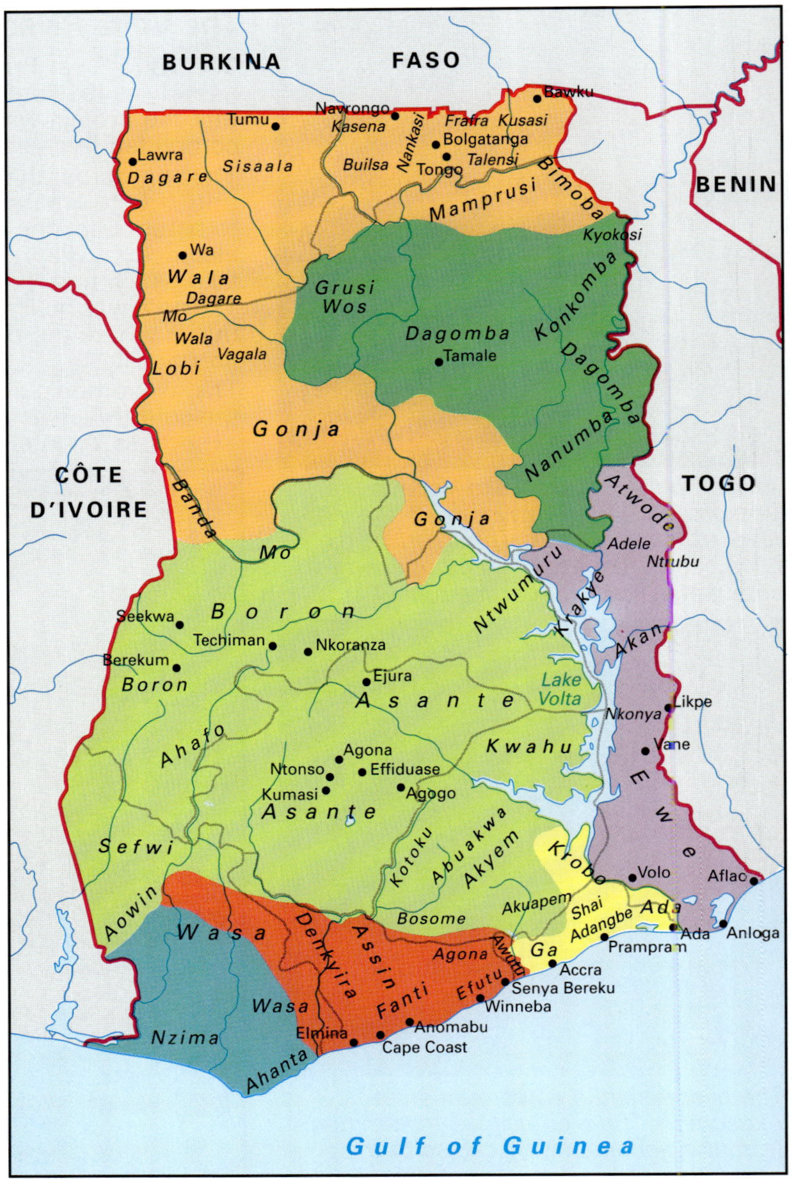

Population

Population density

People per square kilometre

- Over 200
- 100-200
- 75-100
- 50-75
- 25-50
- 0-25

Population of Towns

- ■ Over 100,000
- ◉ 50,000-100,000
- • 25,000-50,000
- · 10,000-25,000

0 50 100 150 200 km

1. *Name three towns with over 100,000 inhabitants.*
2. *Why does the Northern region have a low population density?*
3. *What is the population density in the town of Kumasi?*

In Accra the population density is high and tall buildings provide homes for many families.

Age Pyramid

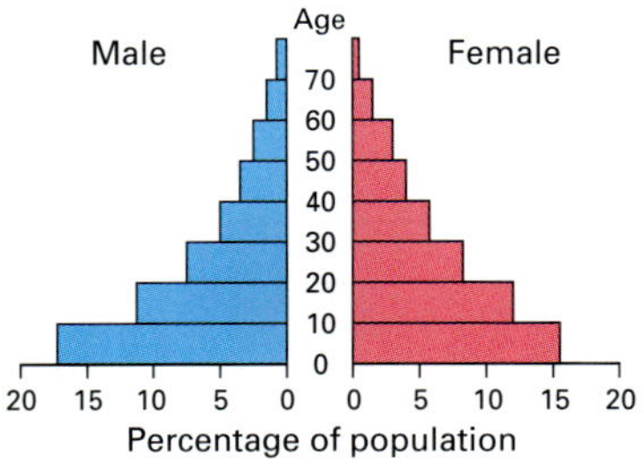

Ethnic Groups and Languages

English is the official language

Major Language Areas

- Akan-Twi
- Akan-Fanti
- Dagbani
- Ewe
- Ga
- Hausa and Moshie
- Nzima
- *Fanti* Ethnic Group
- • Town with Festival

0 50 100 150 200 km

Major Festivals in Ghana

MONTH	FESTIVAL	TOWN, PEOPLE OR REGION
January	Rice festival	Akpafu people
	Kwafie	Berekum
	Ntoa Fokuokese	Nkoranza
	Kpini-Kyiu	Wa
	Danso Abaim Afahye	Techiman
	Tengbana	Tongo
	Jimbenti	Tumu
	Adae Kese	Kumasi
February	Damba	Wa
	Amu	Vane
March	Volo	Volo
	Lekoyi	Likpe
	Lalue Kpledo	Prampram
	Sigi	Navrongo
	Golgu	Bolgatanga
	Kyiu Sung	Upper west and east regions
March/April	Kotokyikyi	Senya Beraku
	Ogyapa	Senya Beraku
April	Dam	Dagomba people
	Bugum	Dagomba people
	Bakatue	Elmina
	Godigbeza	Aflao
May	Don	Bolgatanga and Bawku
	Aboakyir	Winneba
	Sallah	Tamale and Tuma
	Chimisi	Bawku
June	Apiba	Senya Beraku
	Dongu	Wa
	Fire festival	Tamale and Bawku
	Begum	Upper west and east regions
July	Dzumbanti	Wa
	Edjodi	Senya Beraku
	Bakatue	Elmina
	Damba	Dagomba people
	Yam festival	Tamale
	Jimbanti	Tumu
August	Bontungu	Anomabu
	Damba	Tamale
	Akumasi	Senya Beraku
	Asafotufiam	Ada
August-Feb.	Odwira	Asante people
August/Sep.	Homowo	Accra and Ga people
September	Akyempin	Agona
	Fetu	Cape Coast
	Yam festival	Volta region
	Yam festival	Effiduasi
	Kobina	Lawra
	Black stool festival	Seikwa
	Odwira	Akuapeni
October	Boaram	Tonga
	Sebre	Lawra
	Daa	Tongo
	Yam festival	Ejura
November	Hogbetsotso	Anloga
	Atweaba	Ntonso
	Odwira	Denkyira people
	Afahye	Agogo
	Yango	Bawku
December	Kpini	Dogomba people
	Fao	Navrongo

Transport **Ghana**

Key

Main Road	Capital City
Other Road	Important Town
Railway	Other Town
Navigable River	
International Airport	
Domestic Airport	
Air-strip	
Sea Port	
River Port	

0 50 100 150 200 kilometres

Road transport is the most important means of carrying goods and passengers in Ghana. Ghana has 39,410 kilometres of roads of which only 20% are paved. There are 286,774 vehicles which use these roads. Look at the map and you can see how Lake Volta acts as a barrier between the north and south.

Write down two ways of crossing Lake Volta with a car.

Many roads become impassable during the wet season because heavy rains wash away the road surfaces and bridges. This creates serious maintenance problems and hinders the transport of cocoa and timber.

Transport is the most important factor in Ghana's economic development. The absence of good roads is a great handicap because of the problems transporting raw materials to the factories or markets.

This table shows the distances between the regional capitals using main roads.

	Accra	Bolgatanga	Cape Coast	Ho	Koforidua	Kumasi	Sekondi	Sunyani	Tamale
Bolgatanga	773								
Cape Coast	165	744							
Ho	169	639	334						
Koforidua	69	709	234	238					
Kumasi	253	520	224	422	189				
Sekondi	237	816	72	406	306	296			
Sunyani	380	450	423	549	316	127	423		
Tamale	611	162	582	477	547	358	654	288	
Wa	707	246	678	775	643	454	750	384	298

How to use the table –

1. Tamale to Kumasi – look down the left column until you find Tamale, then read across the row to Kumasi and you will see that the distance is 358 kilometres.
2. *Now see if you can work out the following distances*
   a) Accra to Wa
   b) Bolgatanga to Ho
   c) Tamale to Sunyani

People and goods can be transported by air, rail, road or water. Transport is essential so that products can be moved to places where they are required; to factories where they are manufactured or to markets where they are sold to the people.

Ghana History

Early History

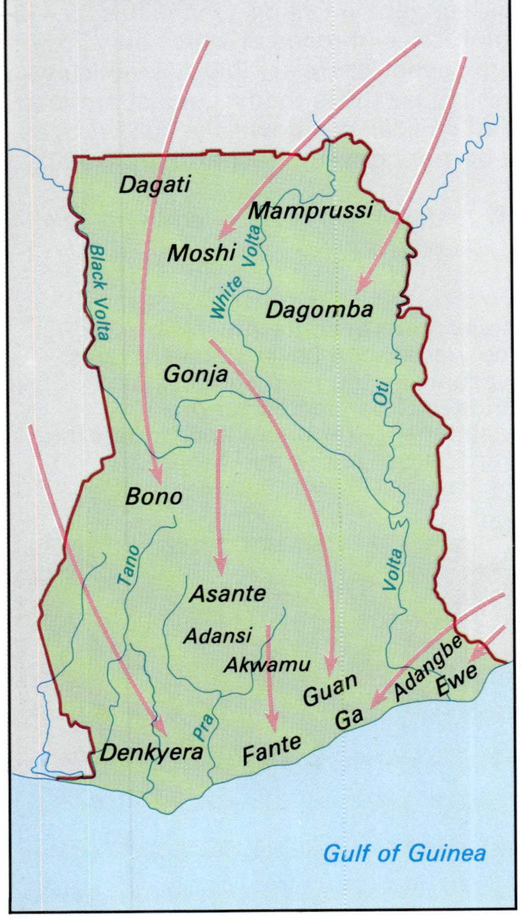

Key

Modern Day International Boundary

Line of Migration

0 100 200 kilometres

From the 1200s, the ancestors of todays Ghanaians began to move onto the land around the Volta. Look at the first map. The Akan people – the Asante, Guan and Fante – came from the north and settled in the central and coastal areas. The Ga and the Ewe came from the east, and the Bono, Moshi and Dagomba came from the north – east.

Can you see where the ancestors of your region came from?

Look at the second map. By the 19th Century many small groups of Africans had joined together to become the Asante empire. This became the most powerful Kingdom in the region. The Asante fought wars to add land to their Kingdom and traded with the Fante people on the coast.

Compare the first two maps. Which groups of people became part of the Asante Empire?

The Asante Empire, 19th Century

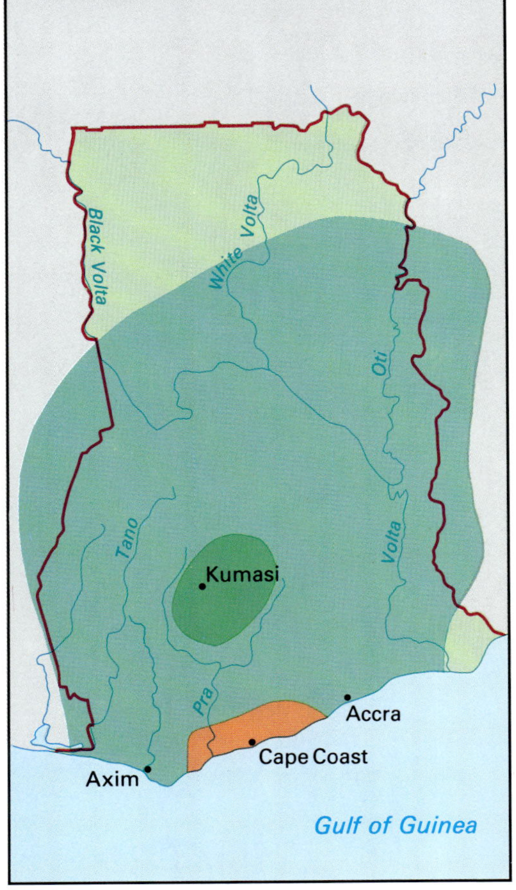

The core of the Asante Empire

The Asante Empire

The Fante states

The Europeans began to arrive in Ghana in the 1450s. When they discovered that there was gold in Ghana they built forts along the coast and began trading with the coastal people – the Fante. The Europeans brought goods to exchange for gold, slaves, ivory and pepper. They called the area the 'Gold coast'.

Look at the third map. Why do you think the Europeans built forts on the coast?

The Europeans fought between each other to gain control of the trade with the Fante. Eventually the British gained control of the trade and of the coastal forts. During the years 1807 – 74 the British fought many wars with the Asante people because the Asante attacked the Fante traders who were under the 'protection' of the British.

Look at the third map and the trade map below it. Why was it so important to the British to keep their control over the traders?

The European Influence

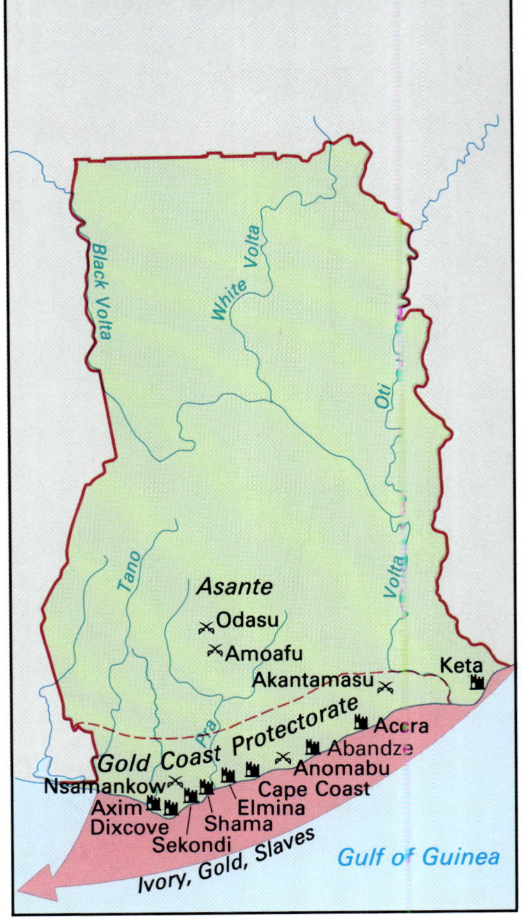

Sea trade

Main European Fort

Asante – British Battleground 1807 – 74

Protectorate Boundary

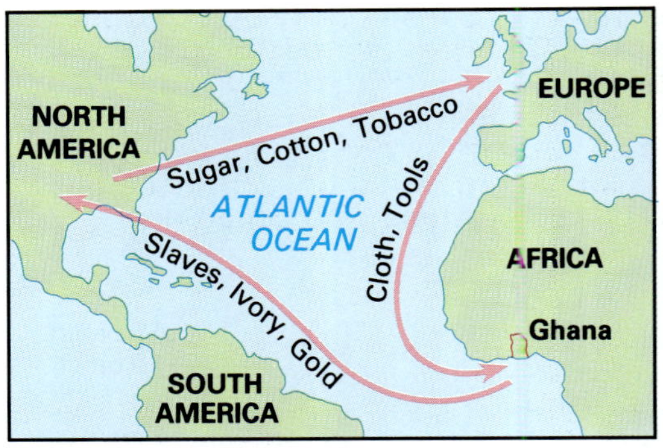

The Trade Triangle

Elmina Castle, the first European fort on the Gold Coast, built by the Portuguese 1481–2. Some of the stone was brought from Portugal.

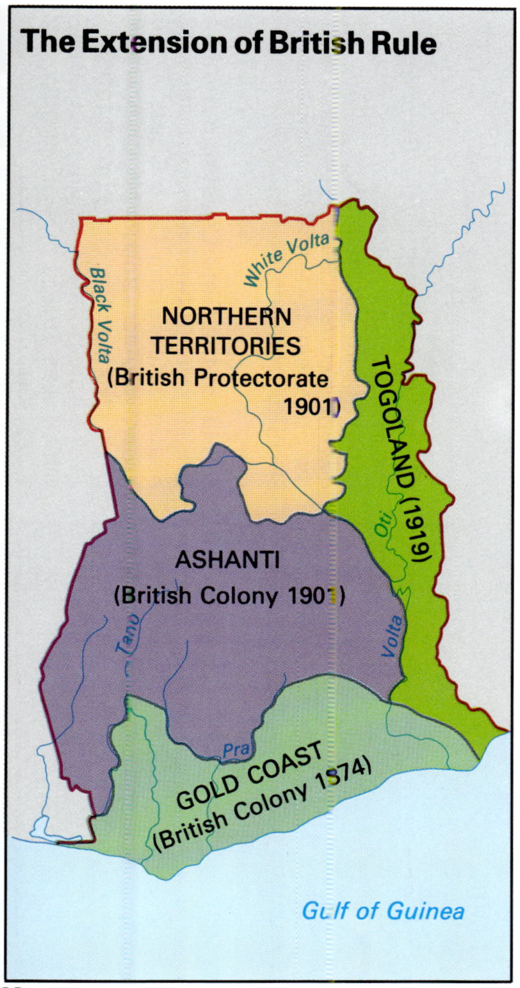

Key

- Modern Day International Boundary
- Regional Boundary

0 100 200 kilometres

Key

- Modern Day International Boundary
- Regional Boundary

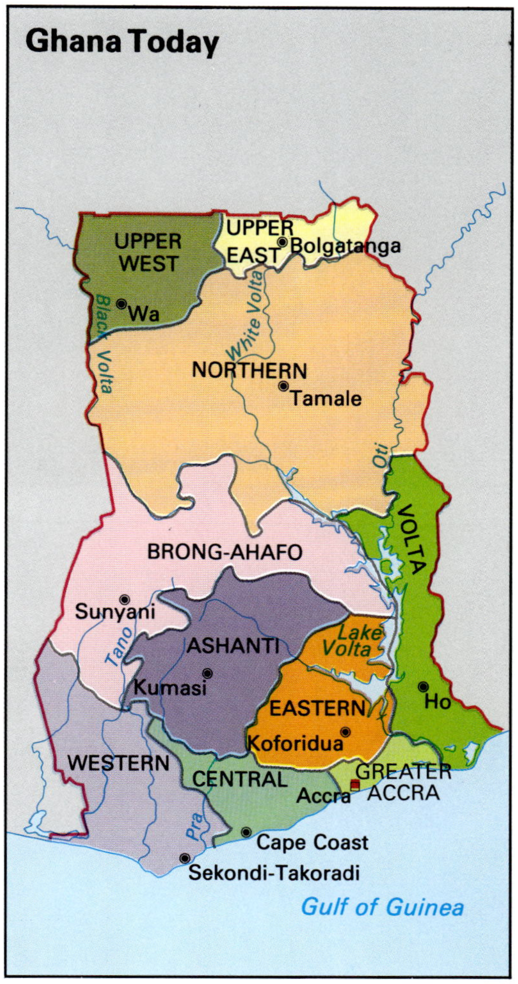

- Modern Day International Boundary
- Regional Boundary
- National Capital
- Regional Capital

In 1874 the British finally defeated the Asante. They proclaimed the coastal area a British Colony and moved inland to extend their rule over the whole country. The Northern Territories, the Asante region and the Gold Coast protectorate became known as 'The Gold Coast Colony'.

Gradually the Africans grew tired of British rule. Economic problems, due to the dependence on a single crop (Cocoa), put pressure on the British to leave. Finally, in 1957 Ghana became an independent nation with Dr. Kwame Nkrumah as prime minister. Under his rule many roads, schools and hospitals were built, Tema harbour was constructed and the Dam at Akosombo resulted in the creation of Lake Volta.

Important Events in the History of Ghana

- 1482 The first European castle is built at Elmina by the Portuguese.
- 1692 The beginning of Osei Tutu's reign and the rise of the Asante.
- 1807 The first of many wars between the Asante and the British.
- 1807 The British abolish the Slave Trade.
- 1821 The British Government takes over the Gold Coast settlements.
- 1874 The Gold Coast becomes a British colony.
- 1877 Accra becomes the capital of the colony.
- 1901 Ashanti becomes a British colony.
- 1901 The Northern Territories become a British Protectorate.
- 1919 Togoland falls under British rule.
- 1957 The Gold Coast becomes independent from Britain and changes its name to Ghana.
- 1960 Ghana becomes a Republic with Dr. Nkrumah as President.
- 1969 The Second Republic is inaugurated with Dr. Kofi Abrefa Busia as Prime Minister and Mr. Edward Akuffo-Addo as President.
- 1979 The Third Republic is inaugurated with Dr. Hilla Limann as President.
- 1993 The Fourth Republic is inaugurated with Flt.-Lt. Jerry John Rawlings as President.
- 1996 Ghana successfully elected a President through the ballot box for the first time since independence after the term of office of the previous Presidency had ended. Flt.-Lt. Jerry John Rawlings was re-elected President for a second four-year term of office on 7th December. At the same time, the second Parliament of the Fourth Republic under the multiparty system was elected to office.

The Statue of Dr Kwame Nkrumah, the first prime minister, which stood in Accra until 1966.

Ghana Accra

Ghana Commercial Bank, Liberty House on Kwame Nkrumah Avenue. Find this road on the map.

Key

- Built-up Area
- Cemetery
- Motorway
- Main Road
- Road
- Railway
- ■ Important Building

0 1 2 kilometres

During the 16th century the Ga people came to live on the coast, where Accra is now built, because of its advantageous position for trade with the European forts and its comparative security from attack.

In 1876 Accra was chosen as the new capital of the Gold Coast and the British moved their administrative headquarters from Cape Coast. The growth of Accra and its population has been striking; the city now extends over 8 miles inland and the population which was 16,267 in 1891 is now 1,222,300

Physical **West Africa**

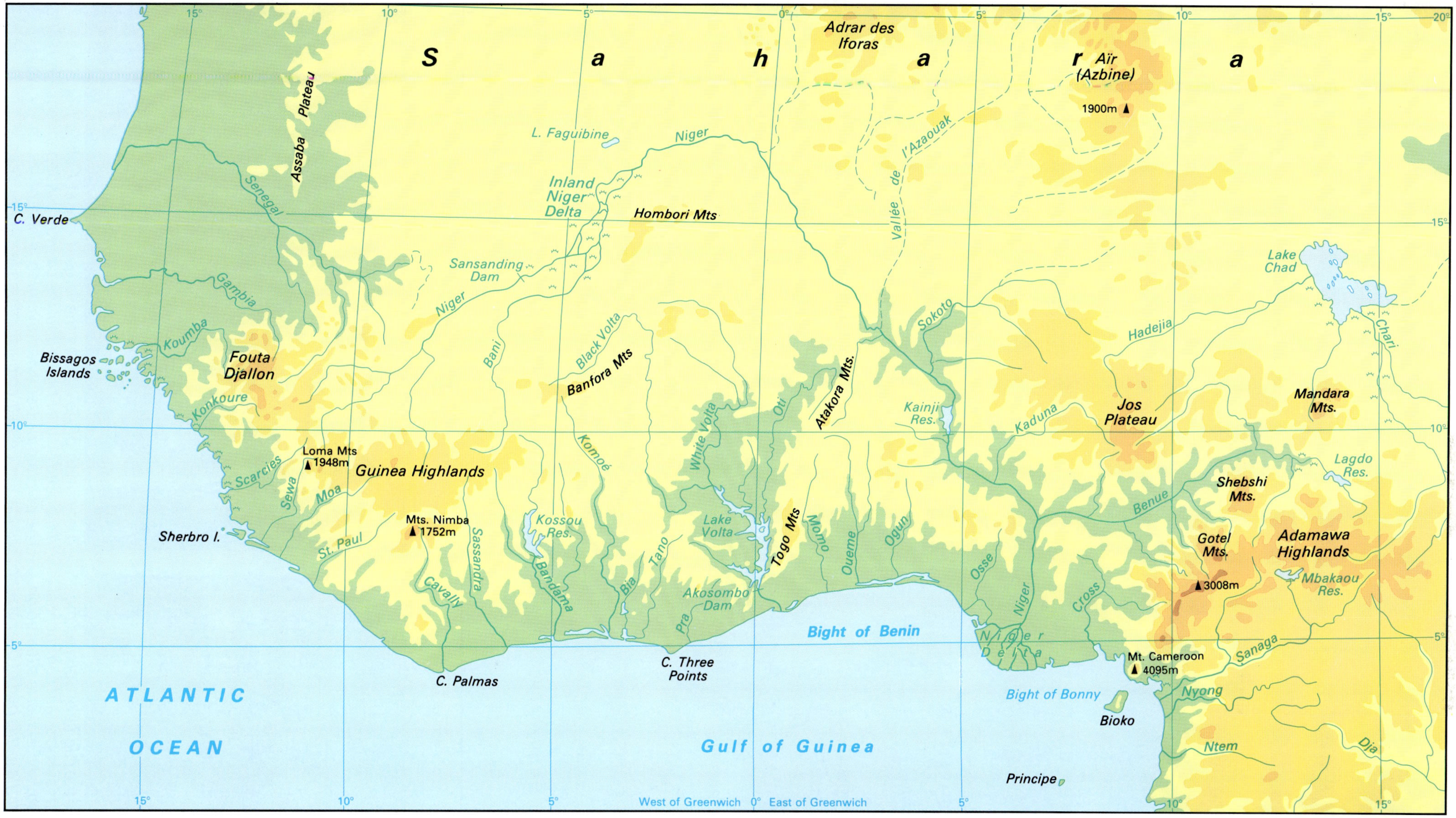

Key

Metres

- Over 2000
- 1000–2000
- 500–1000
- 200–500
- 0–200
- ▲ Mountain Peak
- Seasonal River
- Dam
- Swamp

0 200 400 600 kilometres

1. *What is the name and height of the highest mountain in West Africa?*
2. *The longest river West Africa is over 4000 kilometres in length – which river is this?*
3. *Which is the largest lake in West Africa and name two rivers which flow into the lake?*
4. *Which river forms part of the Ghana international boundary?*
5. *What is the largest island in the Gulf of Guinea?*

Sahara Desert,Mauritania.How many other deserts are there in Africa? Name them.

Jos Plateau,Nigeria.This is a major upland feature,from the legend find its height.Name two other upland areas.

West Africa Political and ECOWAS

Key

0 100 200 300 400 500 600 kilometres

International Boundary

Capital City

The central business district of Dakar. As the capital of Senegal the city has government offices and as the most important commercial centre and port it has many business premises. Dakar is situated on many ocean routes and handles all the traffic in this part of the Atlantic.

The growth of Abidjan as the largest city in Côte d'Ivoire was influenced by the French until the country's independence in 1960. The planting of tree-lined avenues is one of the many ways in which the French colonial influence can be seen.

◉ Important Town ○ Other Town

Countries belonging to ECOWAS

The Economic Community of West African States (ECOWAS)

The community was formed in 1975 with the object of promoting trade, co-operation and self-reliance in West Africa. There are two representatives from each country and the headquarters are in Abuja, Nigeria.

The aims of the community are to:

1. Improve relations among members and raise standards of living.
2. Encourage free movement of people, services and capital across international boundaries.
3. Joint development of agricultural, economic and industrial policies; eliminate the large differences in levels of development.
4. Promote common projects such as the exploitation of natural resources.
5. Development of a regional transport network; improve road and rail links between members.
6. Common monetary policy.
7. Form a common market by 1990 eliminating tariffs and other obstructions to trade between members. This is an example of how Ghana could benefit from this – the aluminium smelter at Tema could use alumina produced in Guinea; then the aluminium products could be traded with other members.

The sports stadium and Independence Arch in Accra. Independence Arch was built to commemorate Ghana's independence in 1957 and the black star above the arch symbolises African freedom.

Areas of West African Countries

Country	Area in sq.km.	Guinea Bissau	36 125
Benin	112 622	Liberia	112 600
Burkina Faso	274 122	Mali	1240 142
Cameroon	465 054	Mauritania	1030 700
Cape Verde	4 033	Niger	1186 408
Côte d'Ivoire	322 463	Nigeria	923 773
The Gambia	10 689	Senegal	196 192
Ghana	238 305	Sierra Leone	73 326
Guinea	245 857	Togo	56 785

West Africa Climate

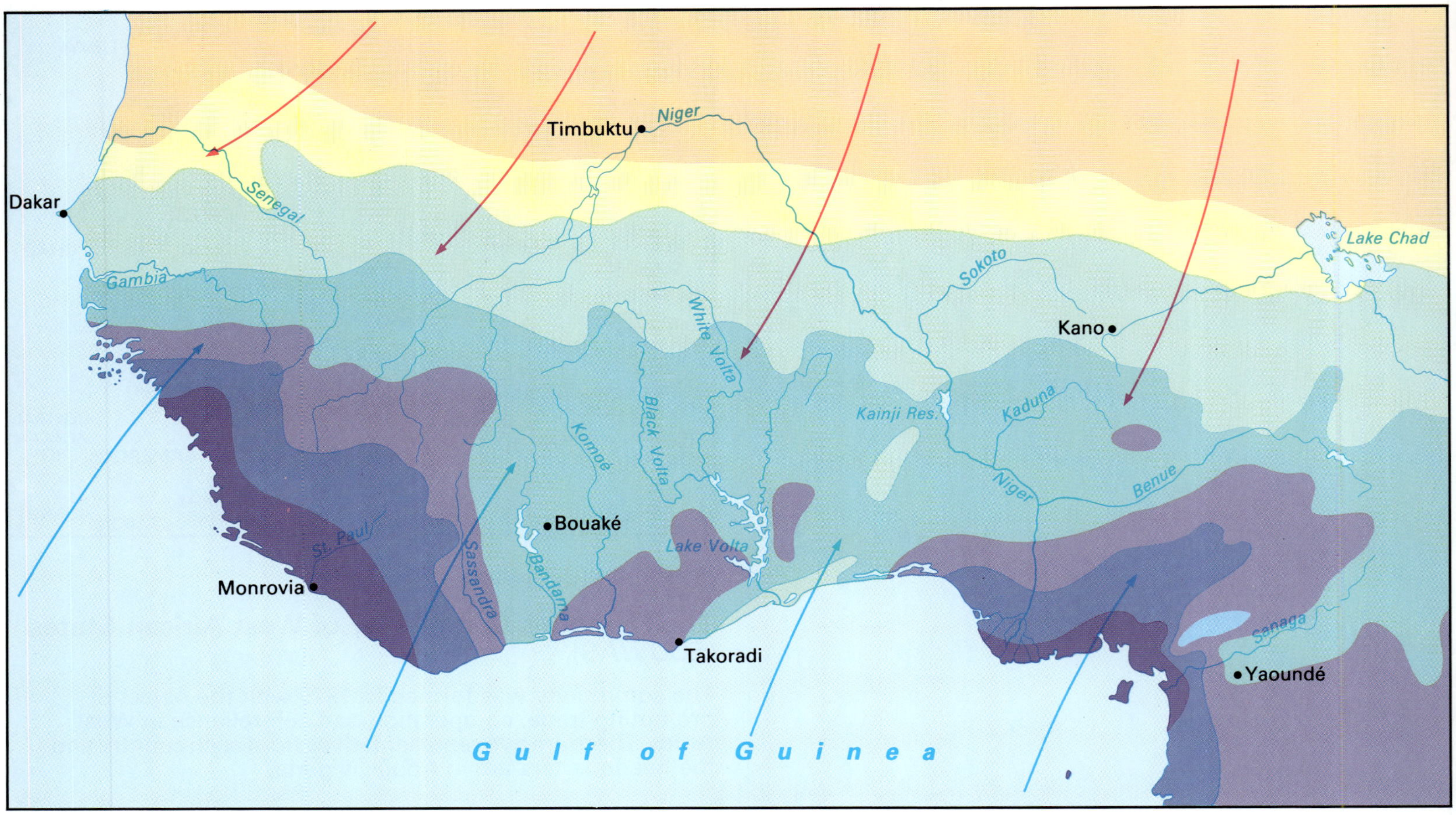

Key

Rainfall in Millimetres

- Over 3000
- 2000 – 3000
- 1500 – 2000
- 1000 – 1500
- 500 – 1000
- 250 – 500
- Less than 250

Prevailing Winds

January
- Dry continental air-Harmattan

July
- Moist maritime air-Monsoon

0 200 400 600 800 kilometres

1. *Which countries receive*
   a) over 3000mm annual rainfall?
   b) less than 250mm annual rainfall?
2. *Which town has the most rainfall? Look at the map on pages 26 – 27 and write down the names of three other towns which receive the heaviest rainfall.*
3. *Which town has the least rainfall? Write down the names of two other towns with a similar amount of rain.*
4. *Which towns have no rain in January?*
5. *During which month is Takoradi wettest? Takoradi has two wet seasons – look at page 11 and explain why this is so.*
6. *Look at the map on page 29 and see what type of vegetation is found in areas with 500 – 1000mm annual rainfall.*

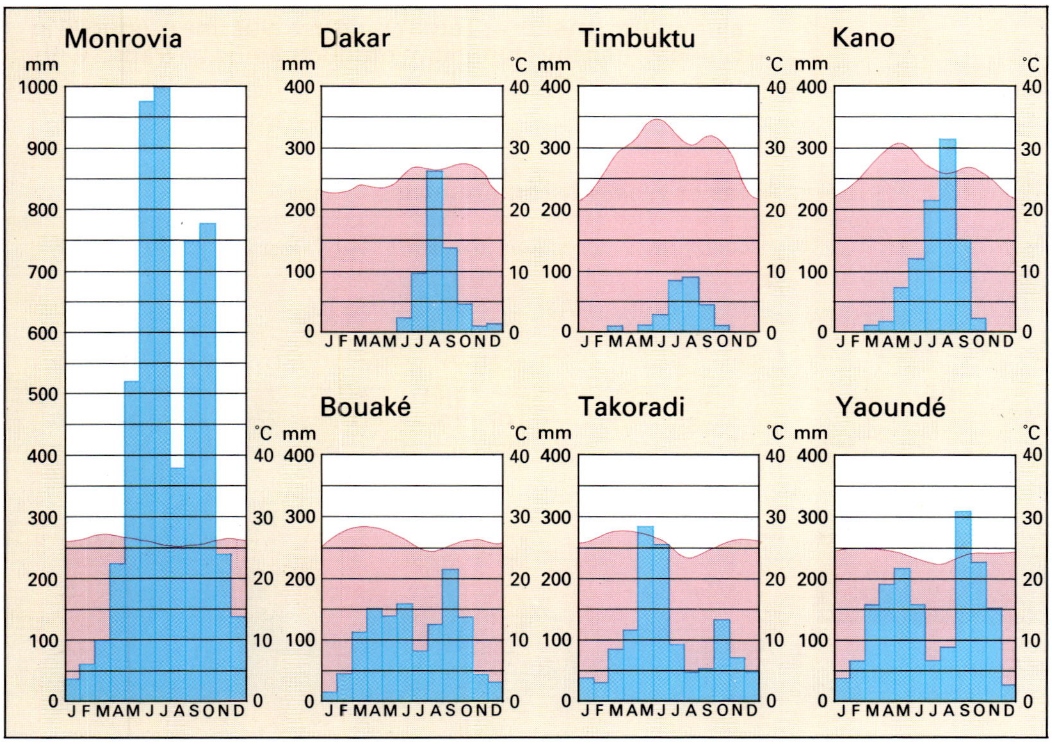

Agriculture is a very important economic activity throughout West Africa. The success of any agricultural activity is heavily dependent upon an adequate and reliable rainfall. This is a major problem especially in the north of the region.

In the areas of heavy rainfall there is the problem of flooding and soil erosion. In contrast there is a long dry season with very irregular amounts of rainfall from year to year in the north of the region. This area has had to suffer severe drought conditions.

Rainfall limits both the type of crops which can be grown and the success of the harvest.

Irrigation schemes are becoming increasingly important in most countries. These schemes enable land to be used where there is inadequate rainfall, for example the Akosombo Dam on the River Volta provides water for irrigation on the dry south eastern plains of Ghana. Water is essential for irrigation – small streams are dammed in the wet season to provide water for crops all through the year.

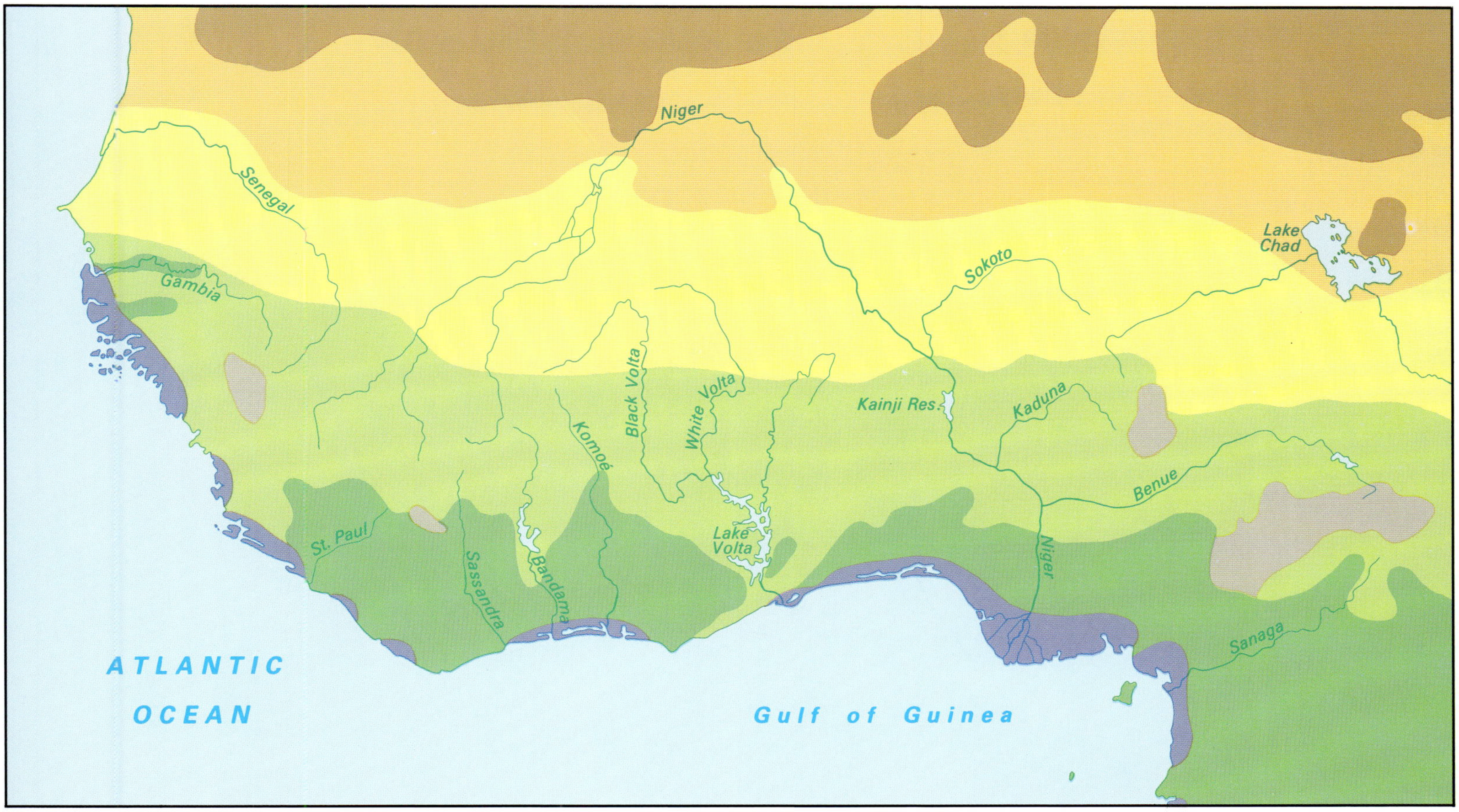

Key

- Desert
- Semi-Desert (Sahel Savanna)
- Sudan Savanna – short grasses with scattered trees and bushes
- Guinea Savanna – tall grasses with trees
- Tropical Rain Forest
- Mangrove and Fresh Water Swamp Forest
- Mountain Vegetation

0 200 400 600 800 kilometres

Desert Vegetation in Mauritania.

In the **desert** the land is bare of vegetation except after occasional rainfall. Poor farming methods and drought threatens to turn many other areas into desert. This process is called **desertification**.

Vegetation in the **sahel savanna** varies from practically nothing in the driest parts to poor grasses and scrub where there is more rain.

The **sudan savanna** has short grasses, which offer good grazing, with scattered thorny bushes and some trees which are mainly acacia and baobab.

Sudan Savanna Vegetation.

Guinea savanna is the transitional zone between the forests and the grasslands. There are more trees and the grasses are taller. Man's need for food has meant the clearing of this vegetation for farming.

What type of crops are grown in these areas?

Tropical rain forest is rapidly disappearing as Man clears it to provide timber and land for cultivation. In the densest forests the trees form a canopy high above the forest floor which allows very little light through for other vegetation to grow.

Swamp Forest Vegetation in the Niger Delta. Where would you find this type of vegetation in Ghana?

Mangrove forest can tolerate salt water and occurs where river estuaries meet the sea. **Fresh water swamp forest** occurs along rivers further inland than mangrove forest and is a combination of woodland and areas of open grassland.

The unique temperature and rainfall conditions that occur with increased height create **mountain vegetation**. On the wetter lower slopes there is rain forest while on higher slopes trees are smaller and grassland appears.

West Africa Food Crops

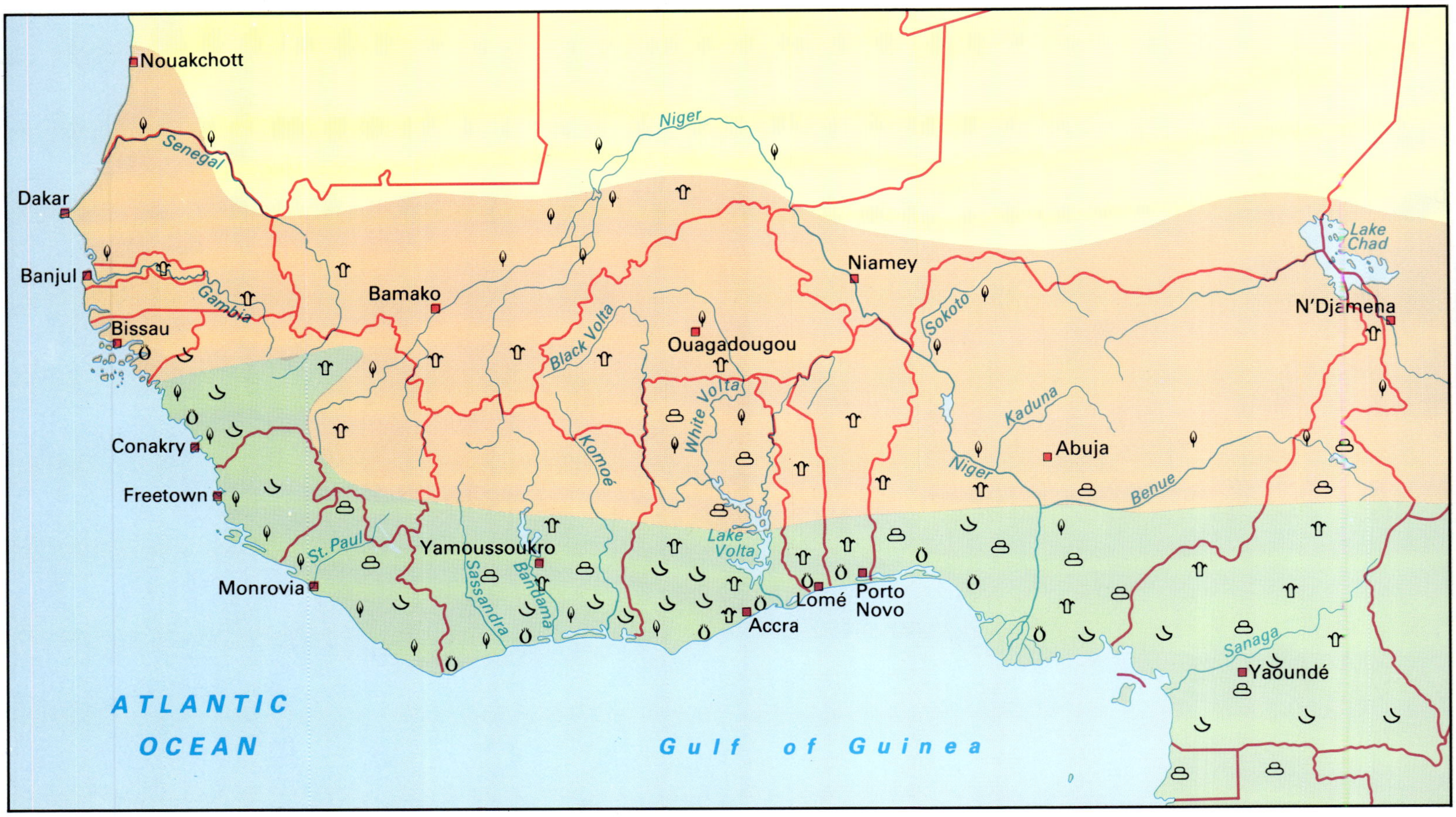

Key

- Cassava
- Millet and Sorghum

0 200 400 600 800 kilometres

- Coconuts
- Maize
- Plantains
- Rice
- Yams

Rice is also an important cash crop

Food Crop Production 1994 – the major producing countries in West Africa

The main aim of most West African farmers is to produce enough food to feed their own families and to have some left over to sell in local markets. This is known as **subsistence farming,** the production of food crops.

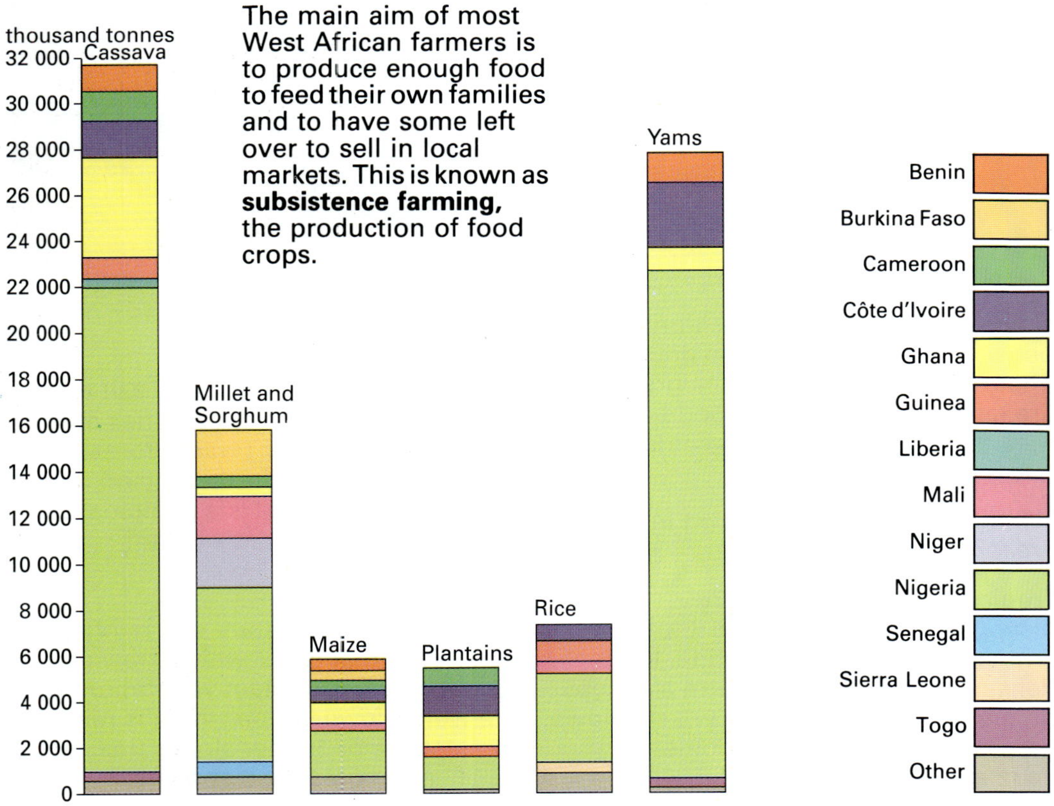

Yam Mounds. At the beginning of the rainy season the farmer makes yam mounds and plants the crop. Millet or maize can be planted later on in the year on the yam mounds and then both crops are harvested at the end of the year.

Market Gardening is important around all the major towns and irrigated regions. The photograph shows that this is a very intensive form of agriculture. The farmer grows some vegetables for his family but sells the majority of his produce at market. The soils are fertilised and watered regularly.

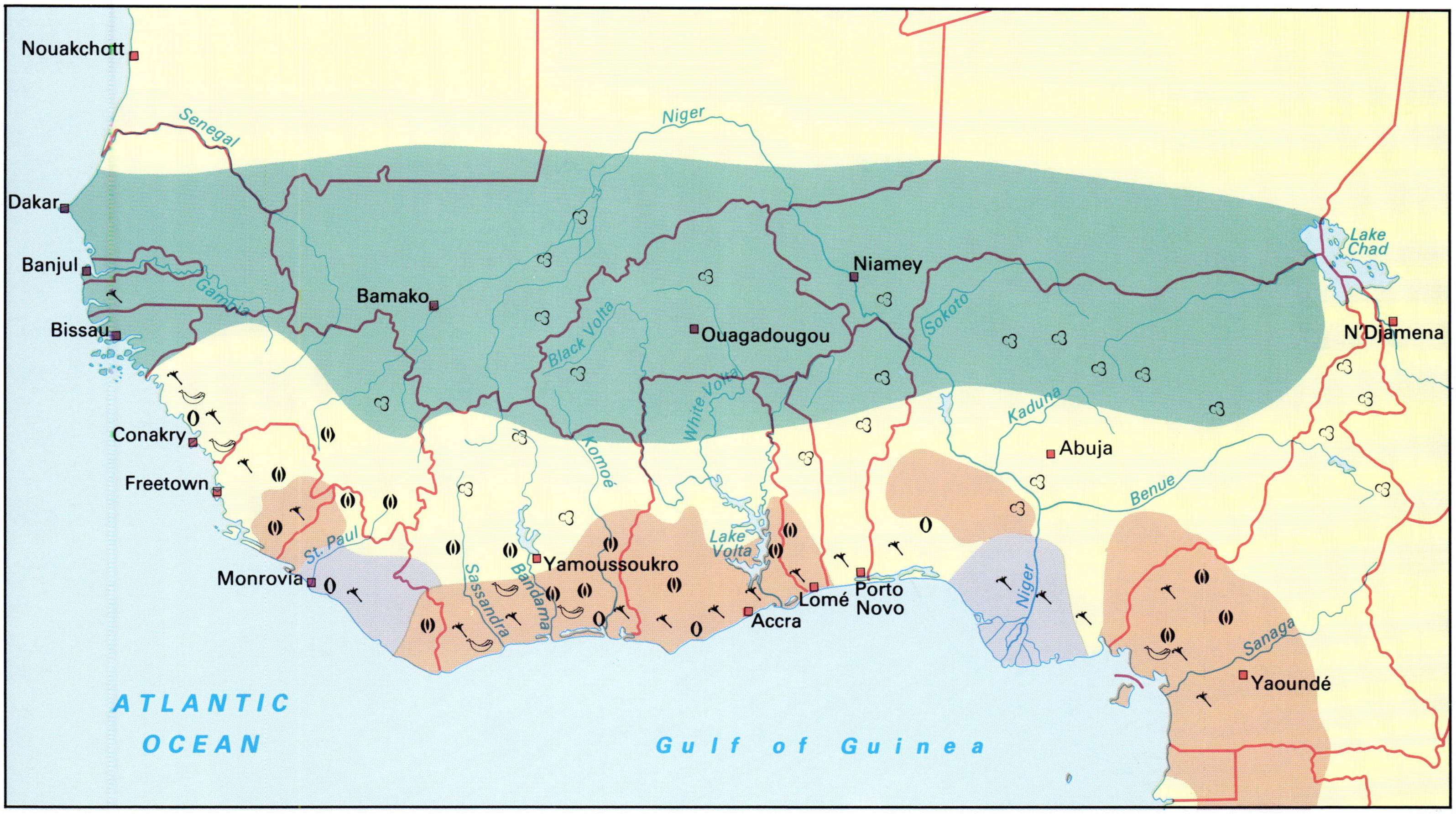

Key

Cocoa

Groundnuts

Rubber

Bananas

Citrus Fruits

Coffee

Cotton

Oil Palms

0 200 400 600 800 kilometres

Groundnuts and Oil Palms are also important food crops

Cash Crop Production 1994

Cocoa

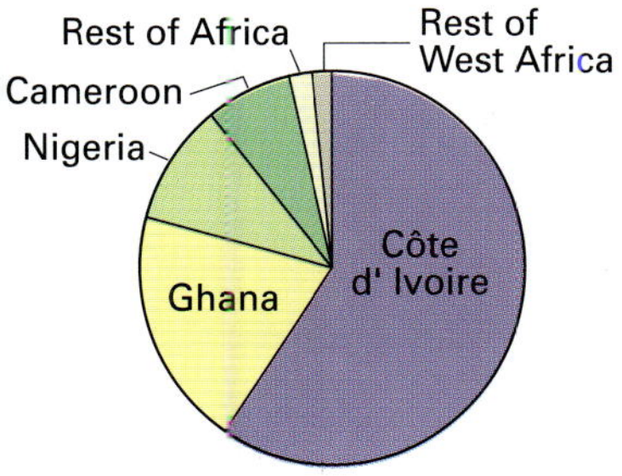

Total:
Africa 1 361 000 tonnes
World 2 564 000 tonnes

Coffee

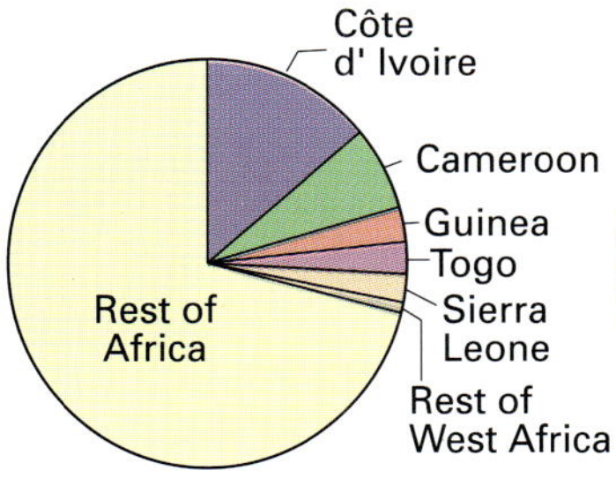

Total:
Africa 1 067 000 tonnes
World 5 430 000 tonnes

Cotton Lint

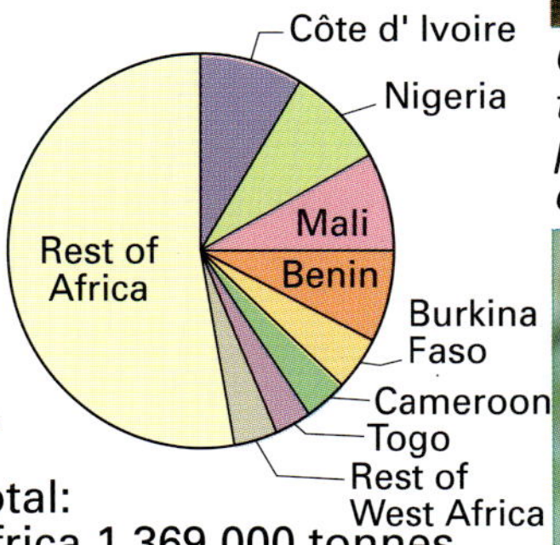

Total:
Africa 1 369 000 tonnes
World 18 425 000 tonnes

Groundnuts

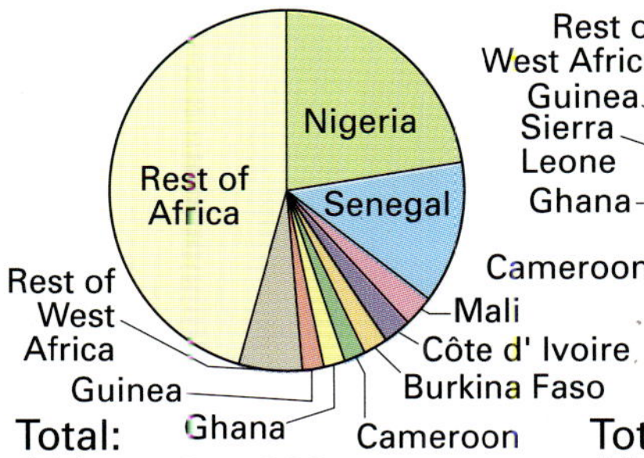

Total:
Africa 5 311 000 tonnes
World 28 493 000 tonnes

Palm Oil

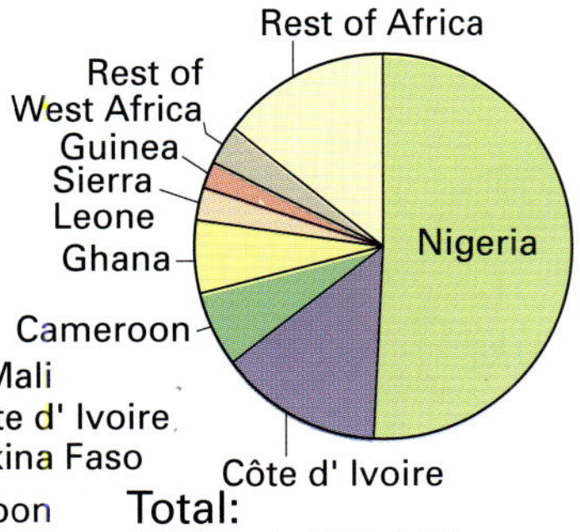

Total:
Africa 1 873 000 tonnes
World 14 577 000 tonnes

Rubber

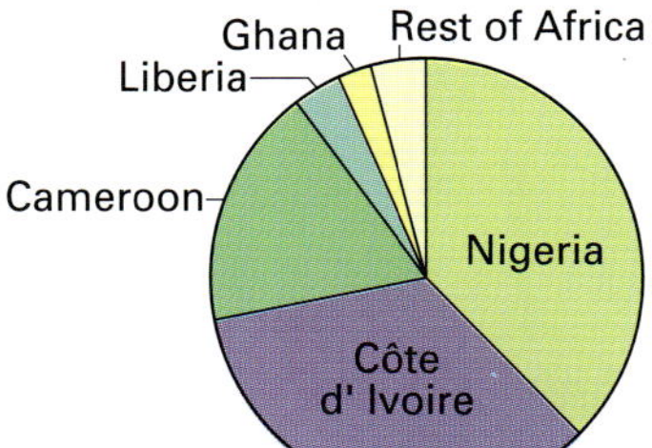

Total:
Africa 281 000 tonnes
World 5 636 000 tonnes

Groundnuts are loaded onto boats and transported along the River Gambia for processing. The nuts are crushed to produce oil which is exported.

Rubber tapping to extract the tree's white sap (latex). The latex oozes out when a cut is made in the bark of the tree, and collected in a small container.

West Africa Minerals and Energy

Key

- Bauxite
- Coal
- Columbite
- Diamonds
- Gas
- Gold
- Iron Ore
- Lead
- Manganese
- Oil
- Phosphates
- Rutile
- Tin
- Uranium
- Zinc
- Hydro-electric Power

0 200 400 600 800 kilometres

The extraction, processing and export of minerals is extremely important for the economy in many of the West African countries.

Offshore oil drilling rig – a long pipe is drilled into the rock through which crude oil is pumped.

Mineral Production 1993

The most important minerals produced in West Africa in comparison to world production.

DIAMONDS **0.7%** — the mineral being produced and its percentage of the world total.

Ghana 10th 700 thousand carats — the country producing the largest amount in West Africa, its placing in the world and amount.

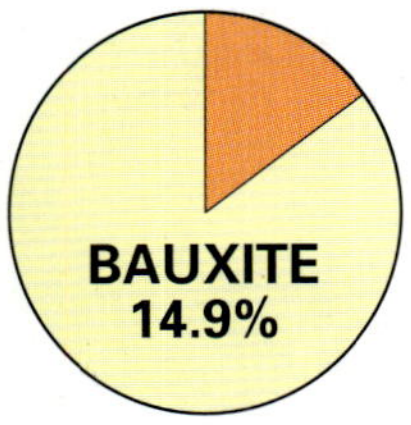

Guinea 2nd
17 040 thousand tonnes

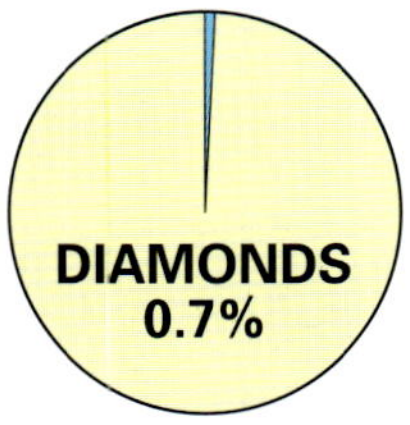

Ghana 10th
700 thousand carats

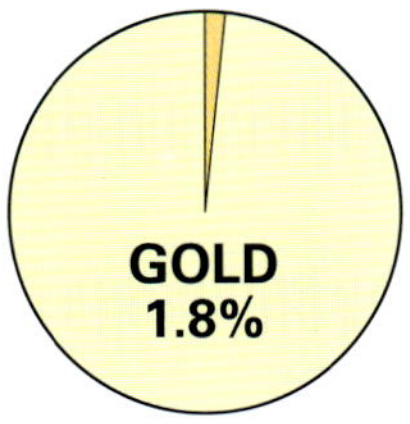

Ghana 11th
41 tonnes

Mauritania 14th
9 400 thousand tonnes

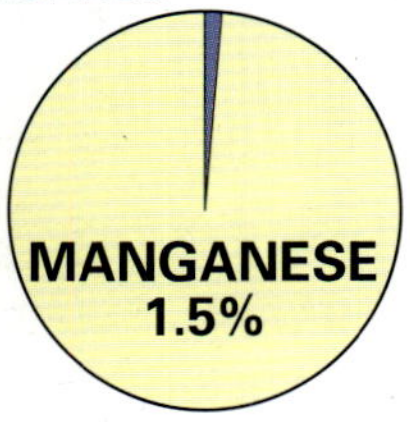

Ghana 10th
107 thousand tonnes

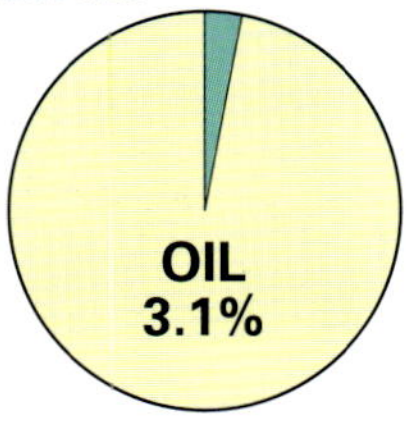

Nigeria 13th
100 000 thousand tonnes

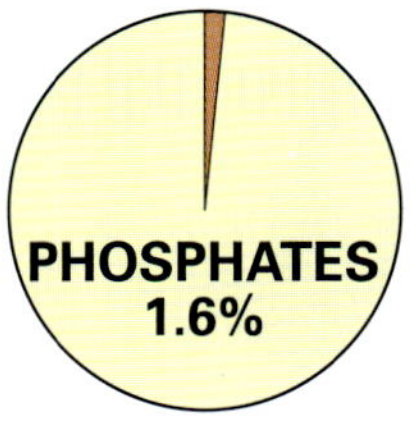

Senegal 11th
2 284 thousand tonnes

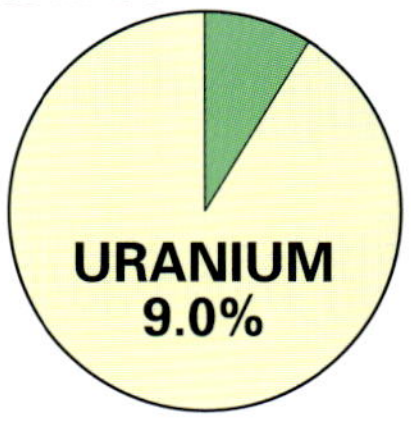

Niger 2nd
2 914 tonnes

Iron Ore mine at Marampa, Sierra Leone. The ore is deposited on the surface before being transported to Pepel for export.

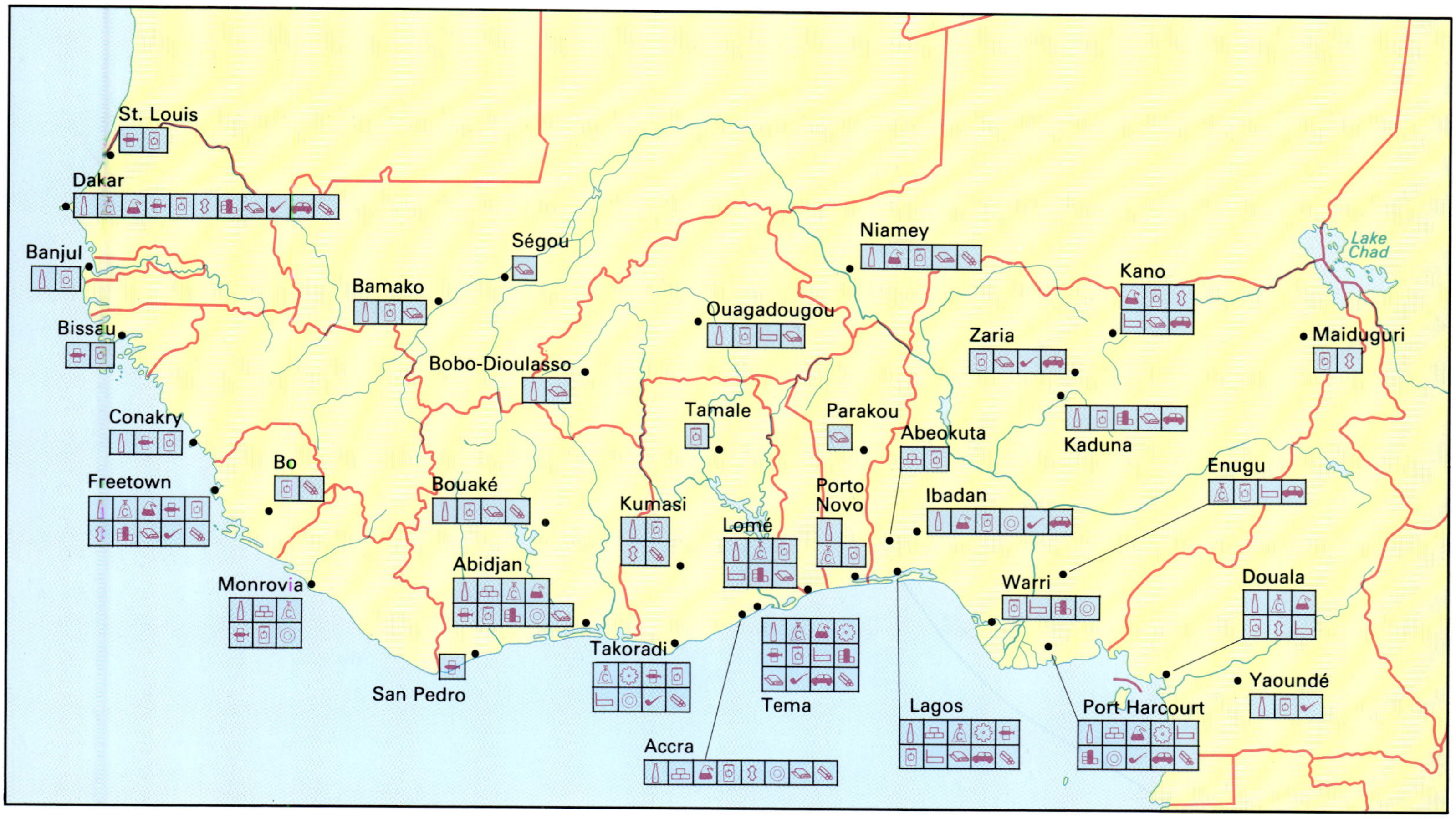

Key

- Beverages
- Building
- Cement
- Chemicals and Plastics
- Engineering
- Fish Processing
- Food Processing
- Leather Goods
- Metal Processing
- Oil Refinery
- Rubber
- Textiles and Clothing
- Tobacco
- Vehicle Assembly
- Wood Processing

0 200 400 600 800 kilometres

1. *a) Name the largest industrial town in Ghana, Côte d'Ivoire and Senegal.*
   b) List the industries of those towns.
2. *a) Why are most of the important industrial centres on the coast?*
   b) Why are there more industries in Accra than Tamale?
3. *Why does every West African country have a food processing industry?*

Oil Refinery in Nigeria using the locally produced oil from the Niger Delta.

Cloth making in the Volta Region, Ghana. Ghana's cotton crop is processed locally at textile mills and by village craft industries.

West African countries realise that there are advantages in greater economic unity such as the development of industries serving the whole region rather than an individual country. As a result **ECOWAS** was created- look at page 27. The graph shows a widening gap between the richer and the poorer countries.

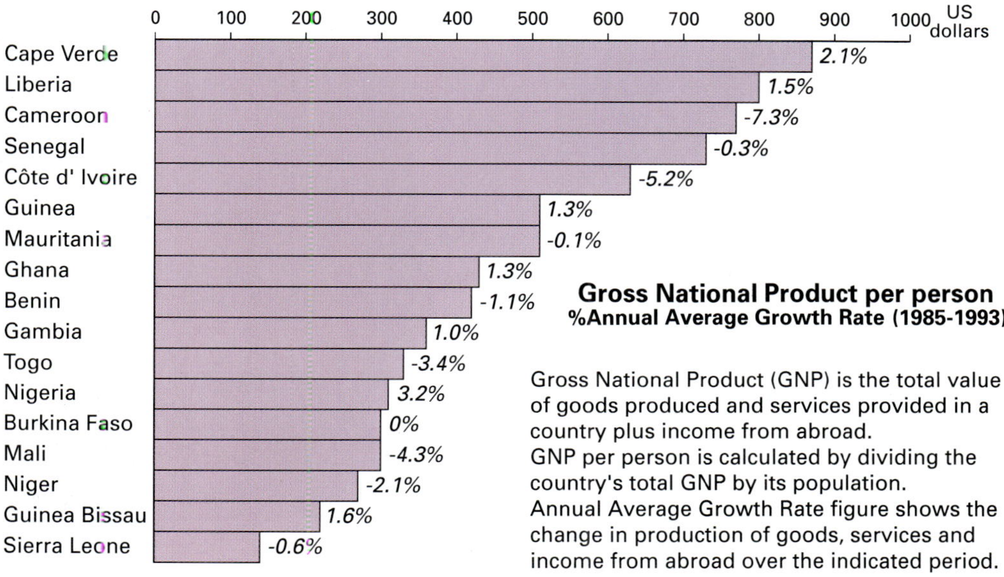

Gross National Product per person
%Annual Average Growth Rate (1985-1993)

Gross National Product (GNP) is the total value of goods produced and services provided in a country plus income from abroad.
GNP per person is calculated by dividing the country's total GNP by its population.
Annual Average Growth Rate figure shows the change in production of goods, services and income from abroad over the indicated period.

West Africa Population and Ethnic Groups

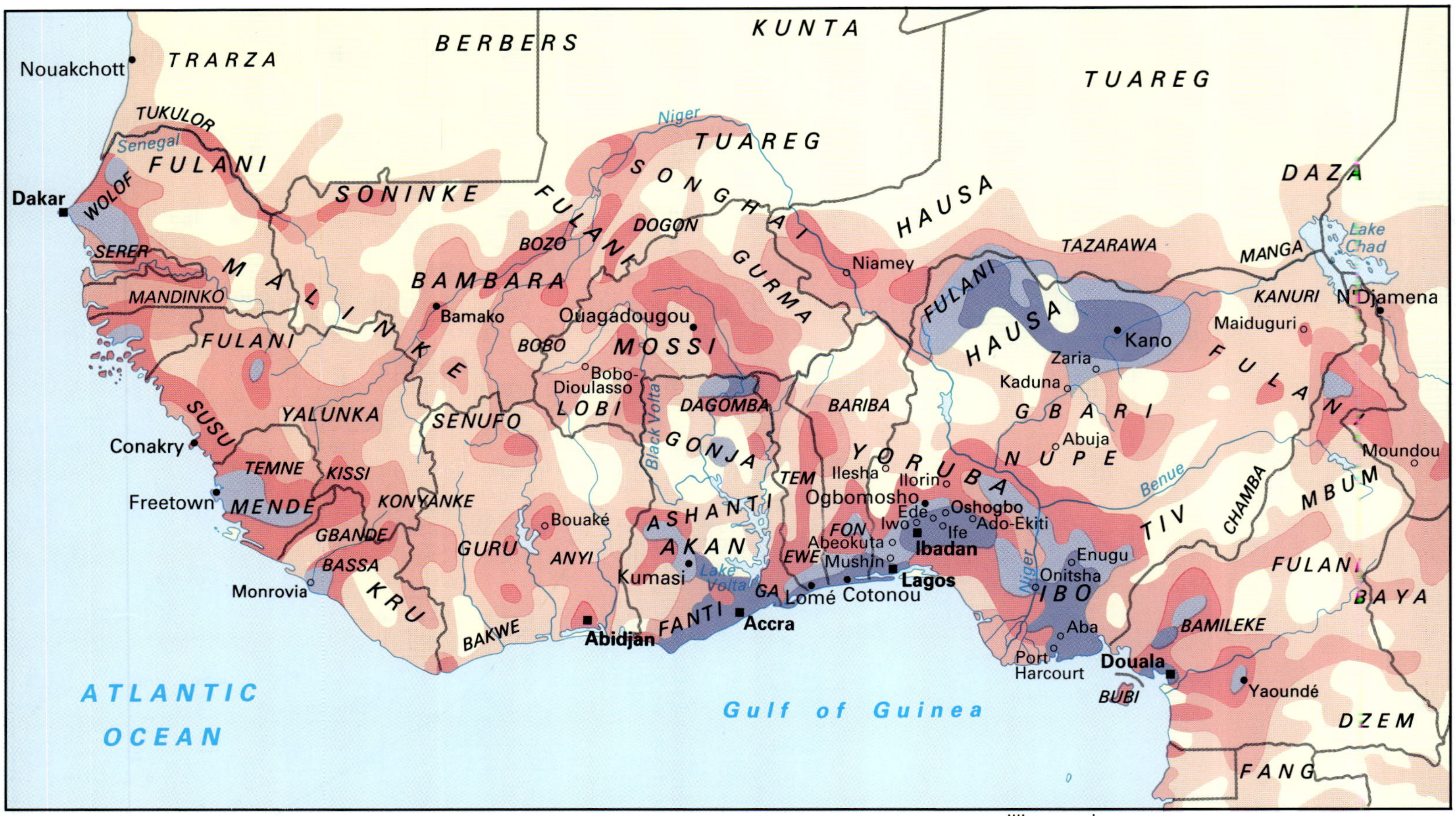

Key

Population Density
People per square kilometre

- Over 100
- 50 – 100
- 25 – 50
- 10 – 25
- 1 – 10
- 0 – 1

Population of Cities

- ■ Over 1 million
- ● 500,000 – 1 million
- ○ 250,000 – 500,000
- *AKAN* Main Ethnic Groups

0 200 400 600 800 kilometres

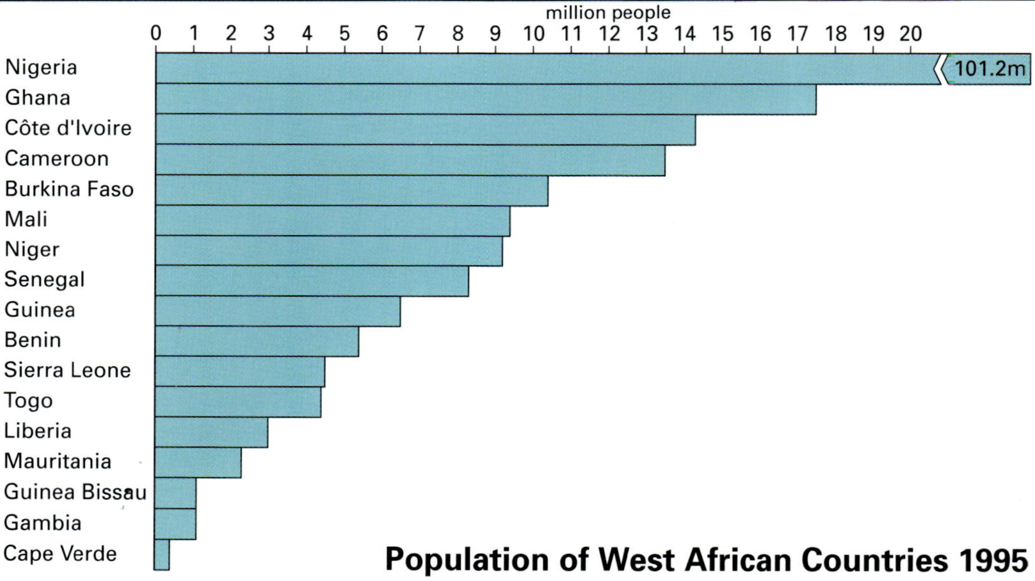

Population of West African Countries 1995

A newly married Fulani couple.

A Wolof Man

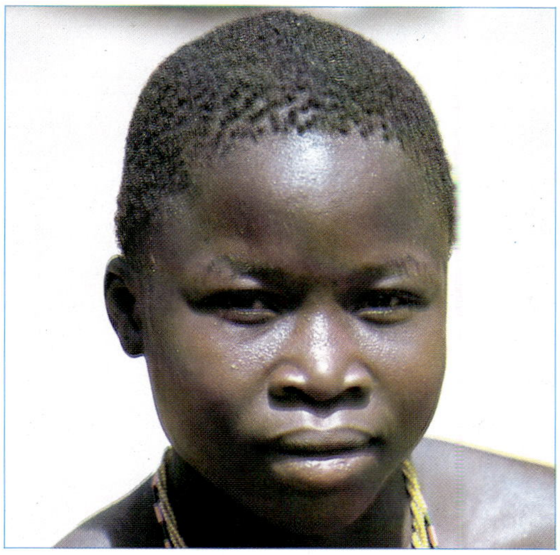

A Lobi Girl

Key

International Boundary	Major Air Route
Major Road	International Airport
Major Railway	Major Sea Port
Navigable River	Capital City
Major Sea Route	Important Town

0 200 400 600 800 kilometres

A dug-out canoe on the River Gambia.

The canoes are still traditionally carved from the huge forest trees. The dug-out canoe is important for the local trade transporting both goods and people to and from the market centres. Canoes are used on all the larger rivers in West Africa and are important for fishing from by line and net.

On which rivers in Ghana are canoes used?

With the creation of the Volta Lake, Ghana is now actively developing water transportation on the lake for cargo transport from Akosombo to Yapei.

The railway station at Takoradi, Ghana.

The railway system in Ghana was developed to serve the gold mines of the south west and to bring cocoa and timber to the coast for export. Ghana's railways still play an important part in her transport network; they carry the whole of the mineral export trade and a large part of the timber and cocoa trade. Passenger traffic has declined with the development of road transport.

Why has the railway network never been extended northwards from Kumasi?

An aerial view of the airport at Kano, Nigeria Many of the airports in West Africa are being improved to take large jet aeroplanes.

Air transport has developed in West Africa because:

a) After independence most countries wanted to develop their own airline.
b) Passengers and cargo can be moved quickly between countries both within West Africa and internationally.

Air transport is economic for the transport of valuable light cargoes but not for bulky cargoes such as minerals.

What is the name of Ghana's international airport and its national airline?

West Africa History

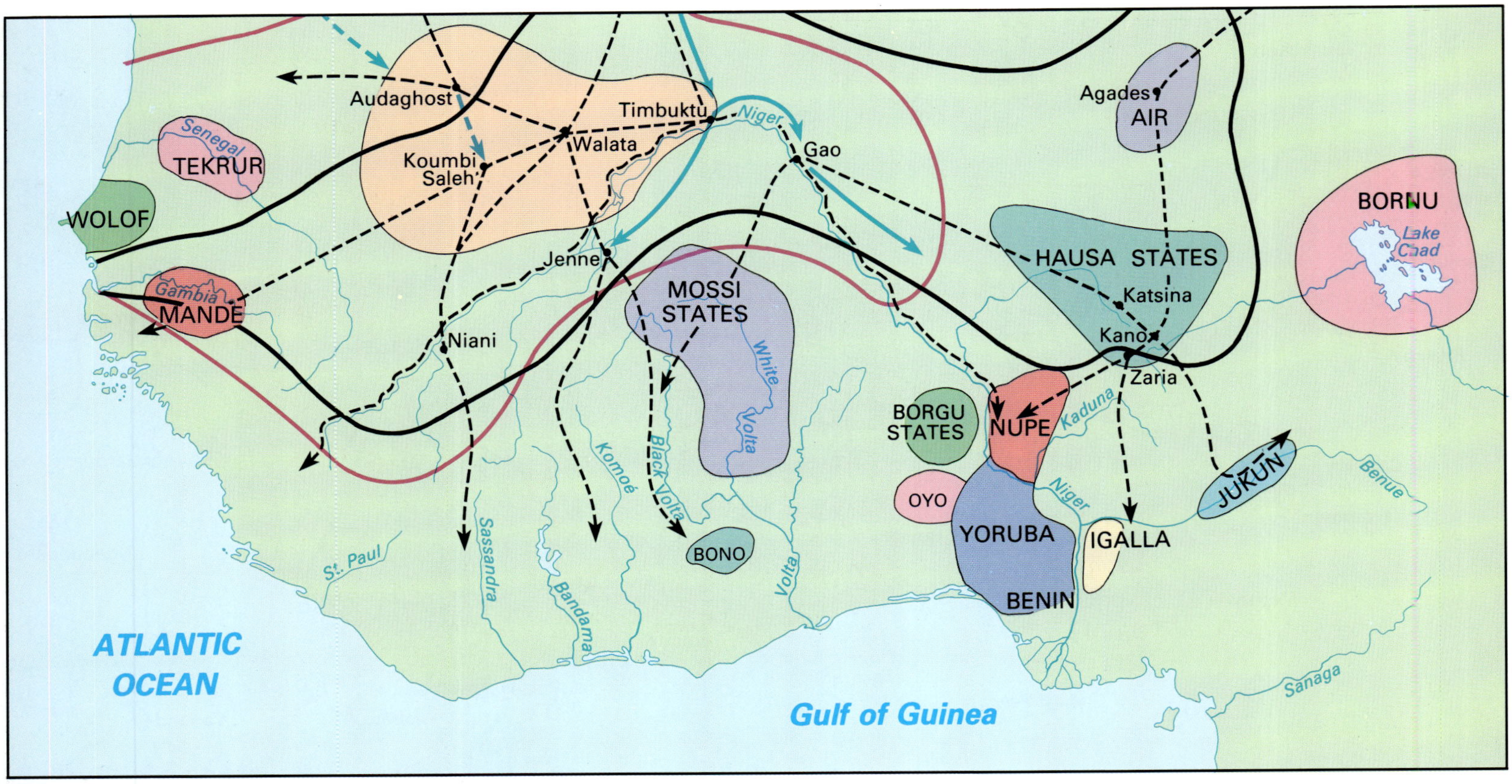

Major States and Empires before 1600

Empire of Ghana 800 – 1240

Empire of Mali 1240 – 1550

Empire of Songhai 1460 – 1600

Trade Routes

Moroccan Invasion of Songhai 1591

Almoravid Invasion of Ghana 1054 – 1076

0 200 400 600 kilometres

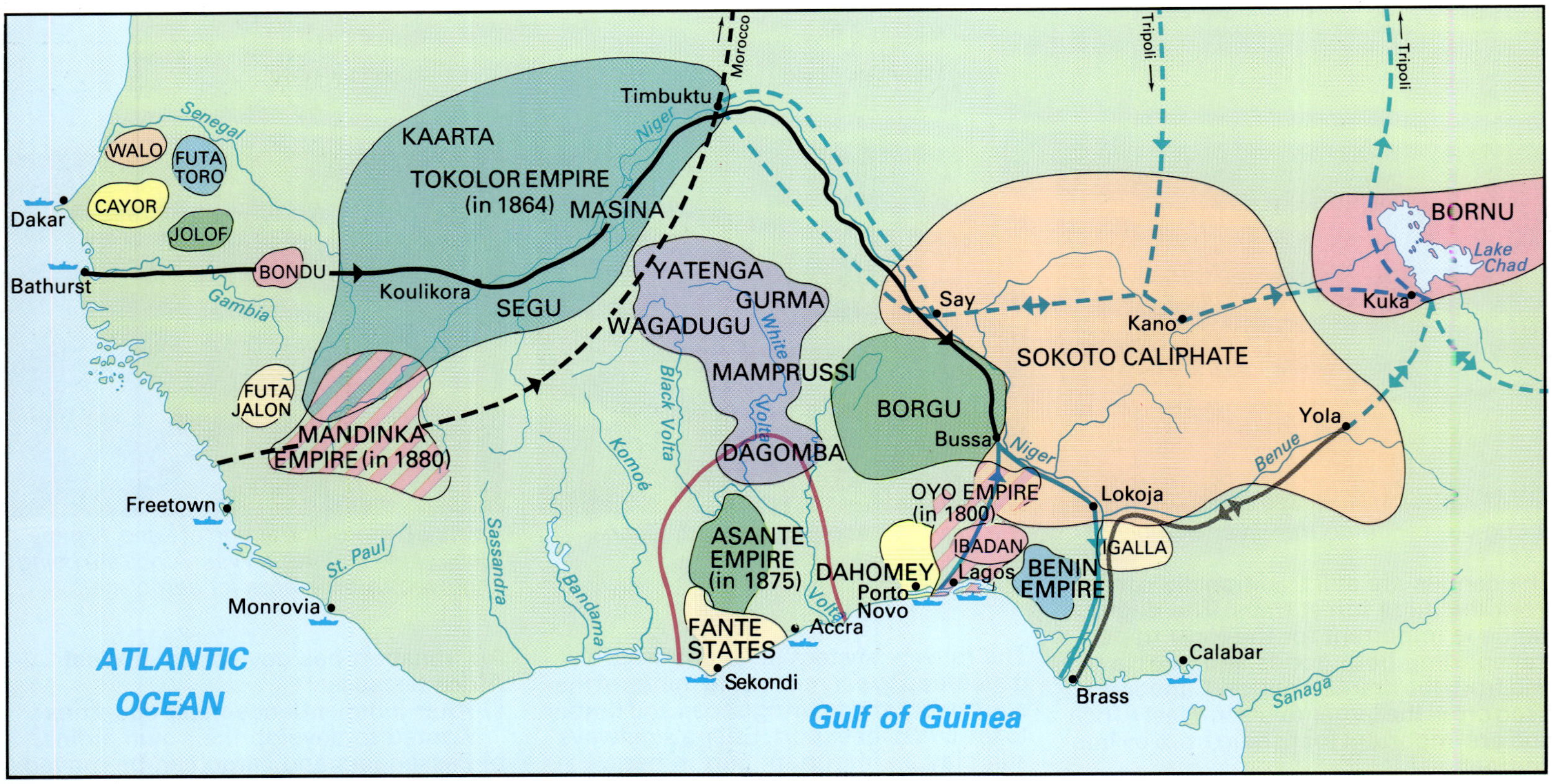

Major States and Empires in the 19th Century

Key

Mossi States

Extent of Asante Empire in 1824

0 200 400 600 kilometres

Explorers Routes

Mungo Park 1826

Calle 1828

R. and J. Lander 1830

Barth 1853

Baikie 1854

Major Port

Physical and Political **Central and Southern Africa**

Key

Metres

- Over 2000
- 1000 – 2000
- 500 – 1000
- 200 – 500
- 0 – 200

0 200 400 600 800 1000 kilometres

- Mountain Peak
- Seasonal River
- Seasonal Lake
- Waterfall
- Dam
- Swamp
- Salt Pan
- International Boundary
- Major Road
- Major Railway
- International Airport
- Capital City
- Important Town
- Other Town

Northern Africa Physical and Political

Key
Metres
Over 2000
1000–2000
500–1000
200–500
0–200
Land below Sea Level
Mountain Peak
Seasonal River
Waterfall
Dam
Swamp
International Boundary
Major Road
Major Railway
Canal
International Airport
Capital City
Important Town
Other Town
0 200 400 600 800 1000 kilometres
ROMANIA
Sarajevo
YUGOSLAVIA
Sofia
BULGARIA
Skopje
FORMER YUGOSLAV REPUBLIC OF MACEDONIA
ALBANIA
Istanbul
Black Sea
Thessaloniki
Bursa
GREECE
Aegean Sea
TURKEY
Izmir
Athens
Konya
Crete
Rhodes
CYPRUS
Sea
Tobruk
Alexandria
Port Said
ISRAEL
JORDAN
IRAQ
Basra
Abadan
Zagros Mountains
Kerman
Zahedan
Suez Canal
Suez
Sinai
Cairo
El Gîza
Cattara Depression
Libyan Desert
KUWAIT
Kuwait
Shiraz
Bushehr
IRAN
Al Jawf
Tabuk
El Minya
Asyût
Nile
The Gulf
Bandar Abbas
BAHRAIN
Manama
OMAN
EGYPT
Qena
Hejaz
Buraydah
SAUDI
Doha
QATAR
Dubai
Abu Dhabi
Gulf of Oman
Muscat
Hofuf
El Khârga
Al Madīnah
Riyadh
UNITED ARAB EMIRATES
Al Jawf
Aswân
Red Sea
Tropic of Cancer
ARABIA
Lake Nasser
Tihama
Wadi Halfa
Jiddah
Makkah
Nubian Desert
Rub 'al Khālī
OMAN
Port Sudan
Emi Koussi 3415m
Karima
Atbara
Abha
Jizan
Salalah
ERITREA
Massawa
Agordat
Asmara
San'ā
CHAD
Omdurman
Khartoum
Kassala
Hodeida
YEMEN
Mukalla
Darfur
SUDAN
El Fasher
Abéché
El Geneina
El Obeid
Gedaref
Kosti
4620m
Ras Dashen
Taiz
Aseb
Aden
Gulf of Aden
Socotra
(Yemen)
Cape Guardafui
En Nahud
Nyala
Gonder
DJIBOUTI
Djibouti
Lake Tana
Blue Nile
White Nile
Ethiopian
Dese
El Muglad
Berbera
Burao
Hargeisa
Sarh
Malakal
ETHIOPIA
Addis Ababa
Dire Dawa
Highlands
Garoe
Wau
Jima
CENTRAL AFRICAN REPUBLIC
Mt. Batu 4307m
Shibeli
Galcaio
Obo
L. Abaya
INDIAN OCEAN
Juba
Juba
Bangassou
Bangui
Uele
Lake Turkana
Moyale
Belet Uen
Gulu
Lodwar
SOMALIA
Ubangi
Bumba
Buta
Isiro
Aruwimi
L. Albert
UGANDA
Bardera
Mogadishu
Congo
Fort Portal
KENYA
Mbandaka
Kisangani
Kampala
Kitale
Entebbe
Kisumu
Meru
Mt. Kenya 5200m
Tsuana
L. Edward
Lake
Nakuru
CONGO (DEM. REP.)
Kismayu
L. Mai-Ndombe
Victoria
Nairobi
Kigali
RWANDA
L. Kivu
Tana
Kindu
Bukavu
Mwanza
Mt. Kilimanjaro 5895m
Arusha
Bujumbura
BURUNDI
Kasai
Sankuru
Moshi
Ilebo
Tanganyika
TANZANIA
Mombasa
Equator
Tana

Africa Physical

Key

Metres

- 2000–4000
- 1000–2000
- 500–1000
- 200–500
- 0–200
- Land Below Sea Level

- ▲ Mountain Peak
- Waterfall
- Dam
- Swamp

0 500 1000 1500 kilometres

The continent of Africa has an area of approximately 30 million square kilometres. The centre of Africa is at least 1500 kilometres from the nearest coast. The landscape is made up of plateaux, large interior basins and mountain ranges.

The highest mountain in Africa is Mt. Kilimanjaro which is in East Africa. Its summit is always snow covered and is 5895 metres high.

Look for Mt. Kilimanjaro in the index.

1 *What is its latitude and longitude? Find it on the map.*

The Nile is the longest river in the world. It flows through North Africa to the Mediterranean Sea and is 6695 kilometres long. Africa's other important rivers include the Congo in Central Africa, the Niger in West Africa and the Zambezi in Southern Africa.

Africa also has many areas of desert, the largest of which is the Sahara.

2 *Which region of Africa does the Sahara cover?*

Key

- International Boundary
- Capital City
- Important Town

0 500 1000 1500 kilometres

Cairo, the capital of Egypt and the largest city in Africa. Find out why Cairo's growth has been influenced by its location.

Nairobi, the capital of Kenya. Kenya has five neighbouring countries, which are they and can you name their capital cities?

Africa Climate

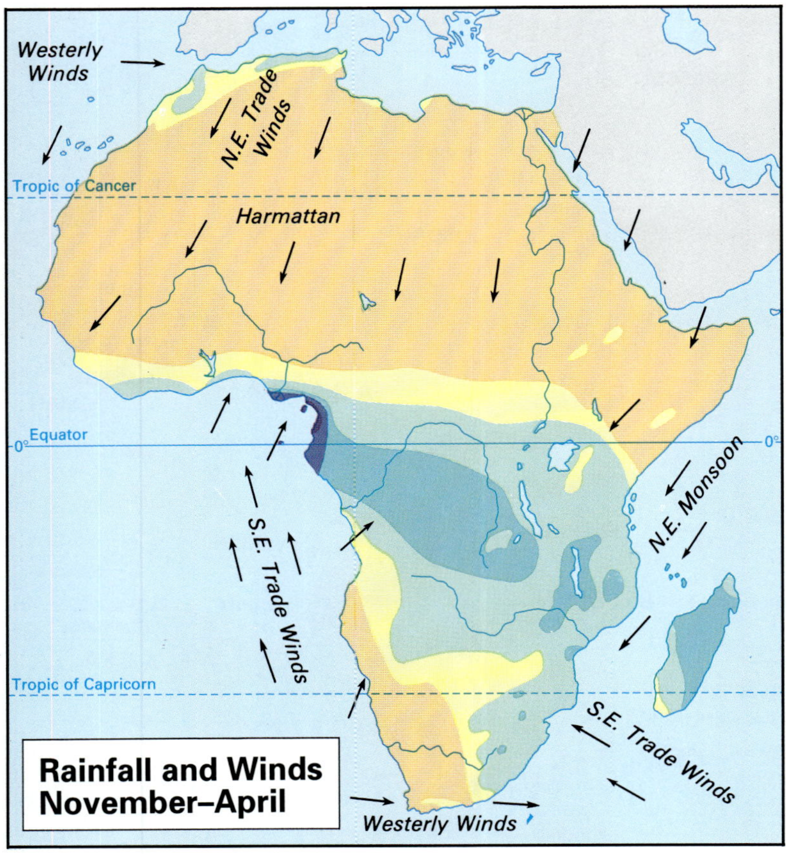

Rainfall and Winds November–April

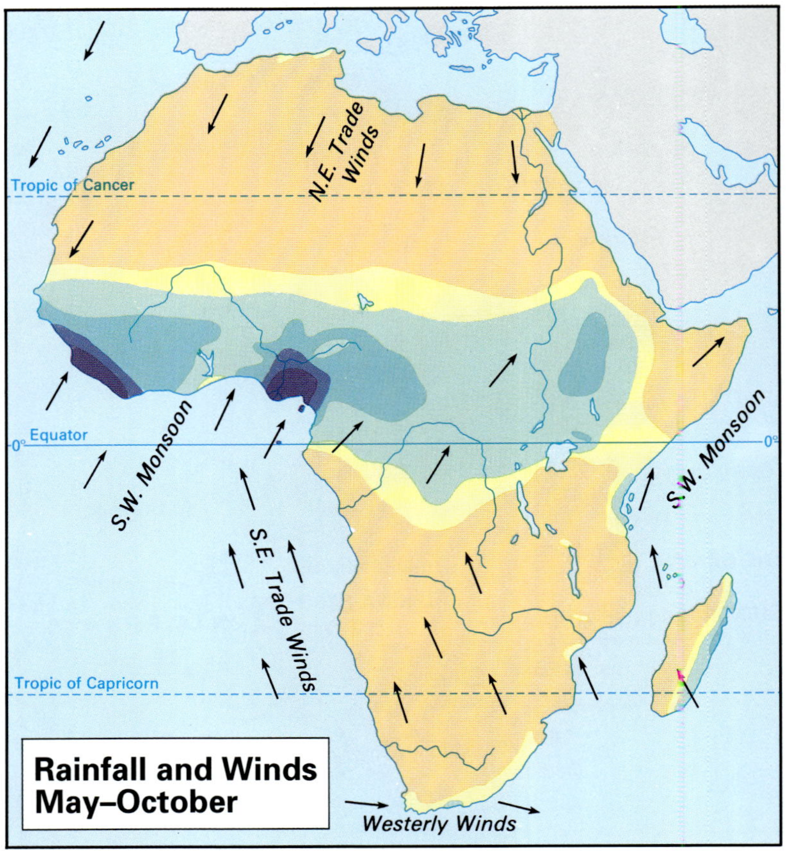

Rainfall and Winds May–October

1 *Which countries receive the least rainfall?*
2 *Why does the variation in wind patterns influence the seasonal distribution of rainfall?*
3 *Why does the amount of rainfall influence the choice of crops which can be grown?*
4 *Look at the map on page 43 and explain the relationship between rainfall and vegetation?*

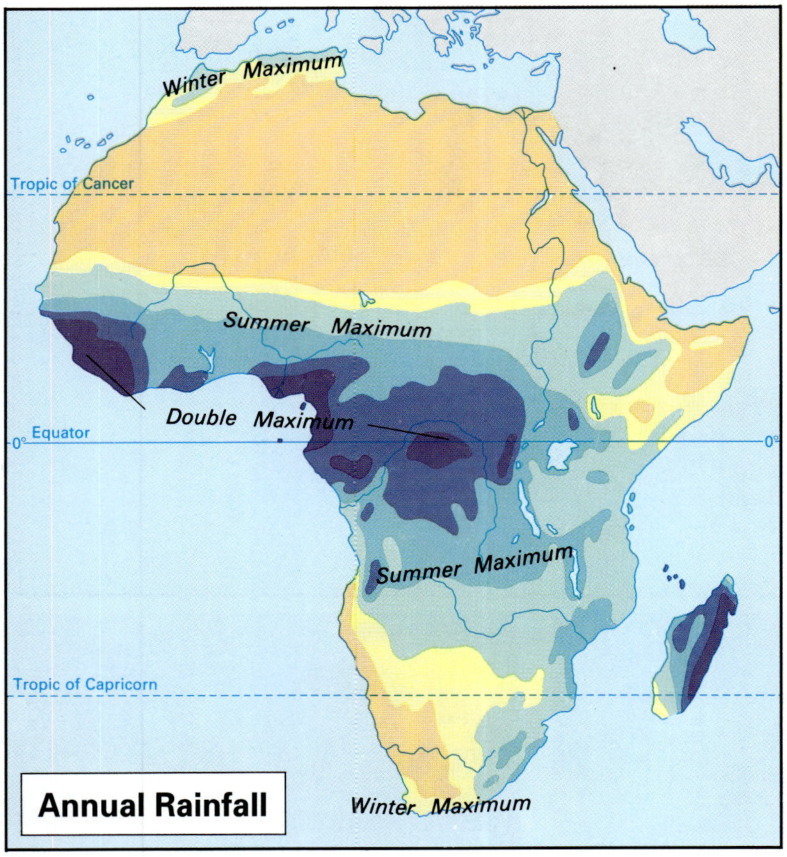

Annual Rainfall

Key

Millimetres
- Over 2000
- 1500 – 2000
- 1000 – 1500
- 500 – 1000
- 250 – 500
- Less than 250

→ Prevailing Winds

0 1000 2000 km

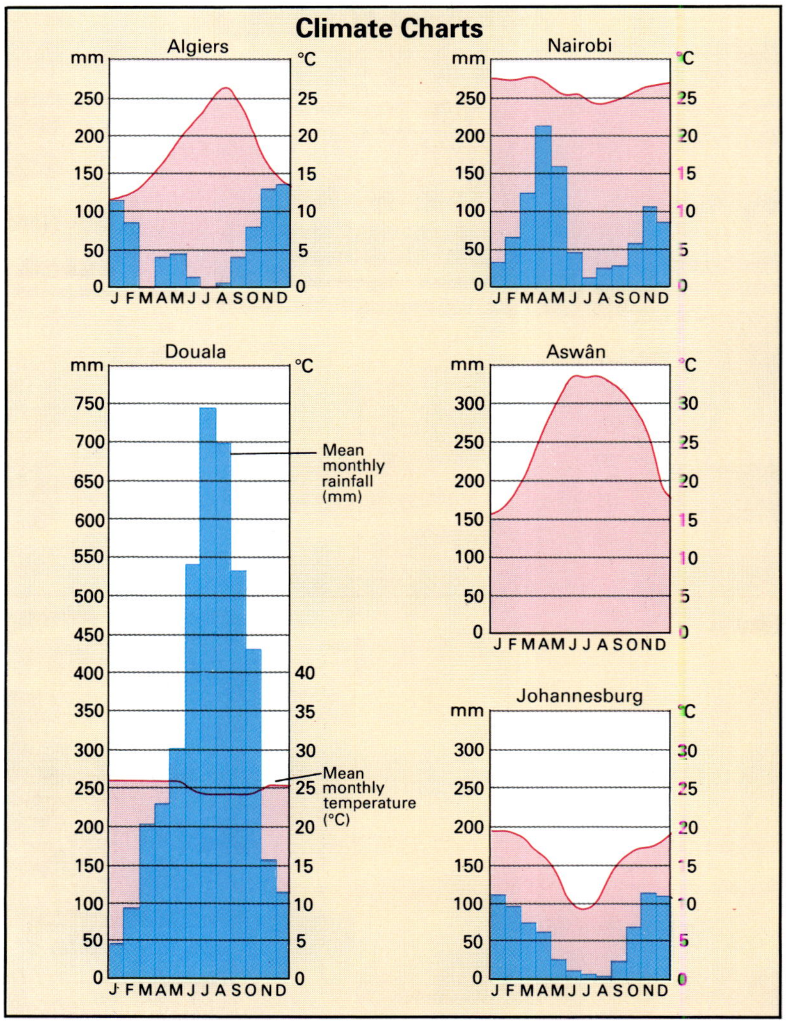

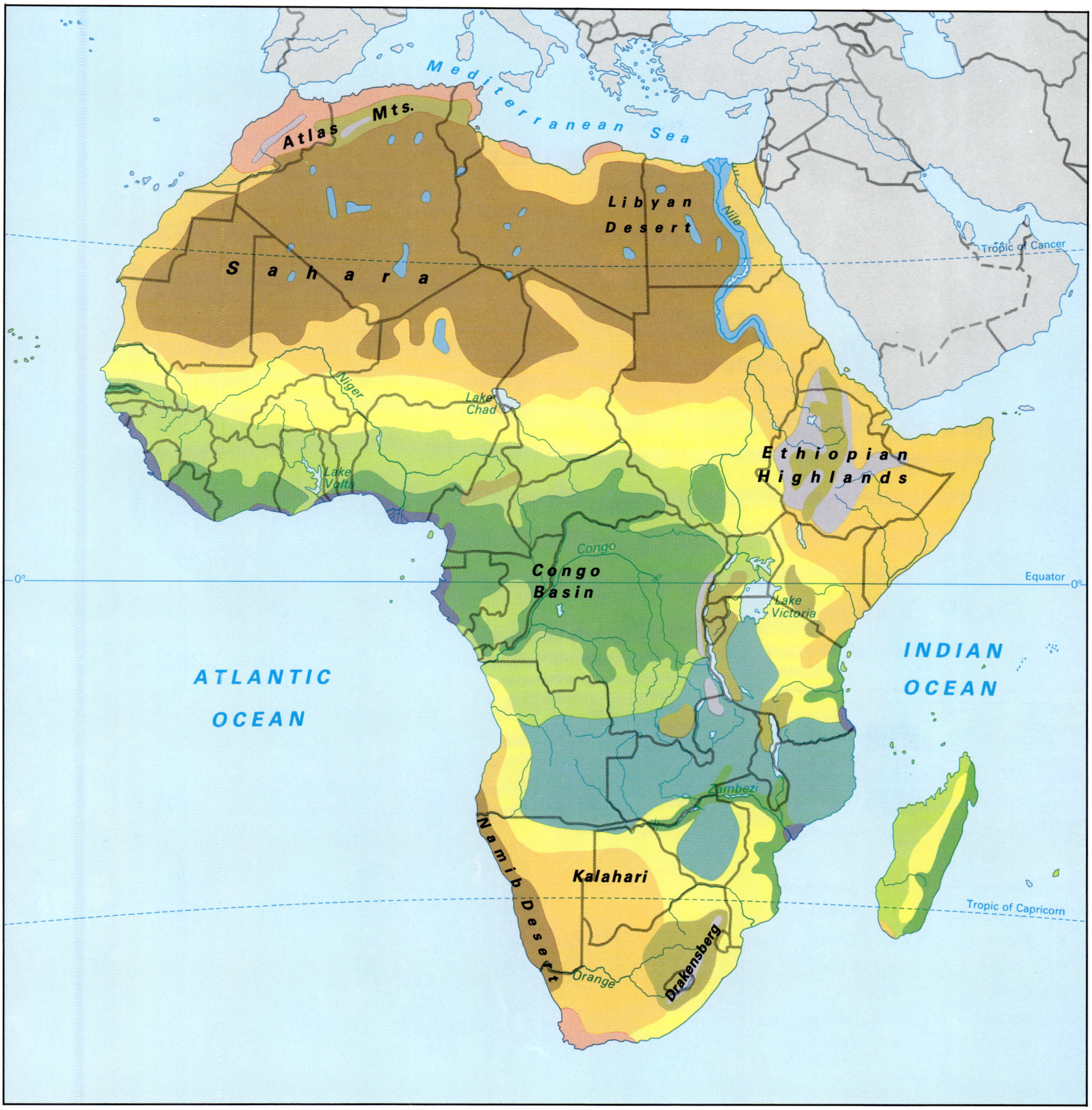

Key

- Desert
- Semi-Desert (Scrubland)
- Short Grass Savanna
- Tall Grass Savanna with some trees
- Dry Deciduous Woodland
- Tropical Rain Forest
- Temperate and Mountain Grassland
- Temperate and Mountain Forest
- Mediterranean Vegetation (evergreen trees and shrubs)
- Mangrove Forest
- Oasis and Irrigated Nile Valley

0 500 1000 1500 kilometres

Short Grass Savanna vegetation with scattered acacia and baobab trees in the Masai Mara Game Reserve, Kenya.

Africa Food Crops and Cash Crops

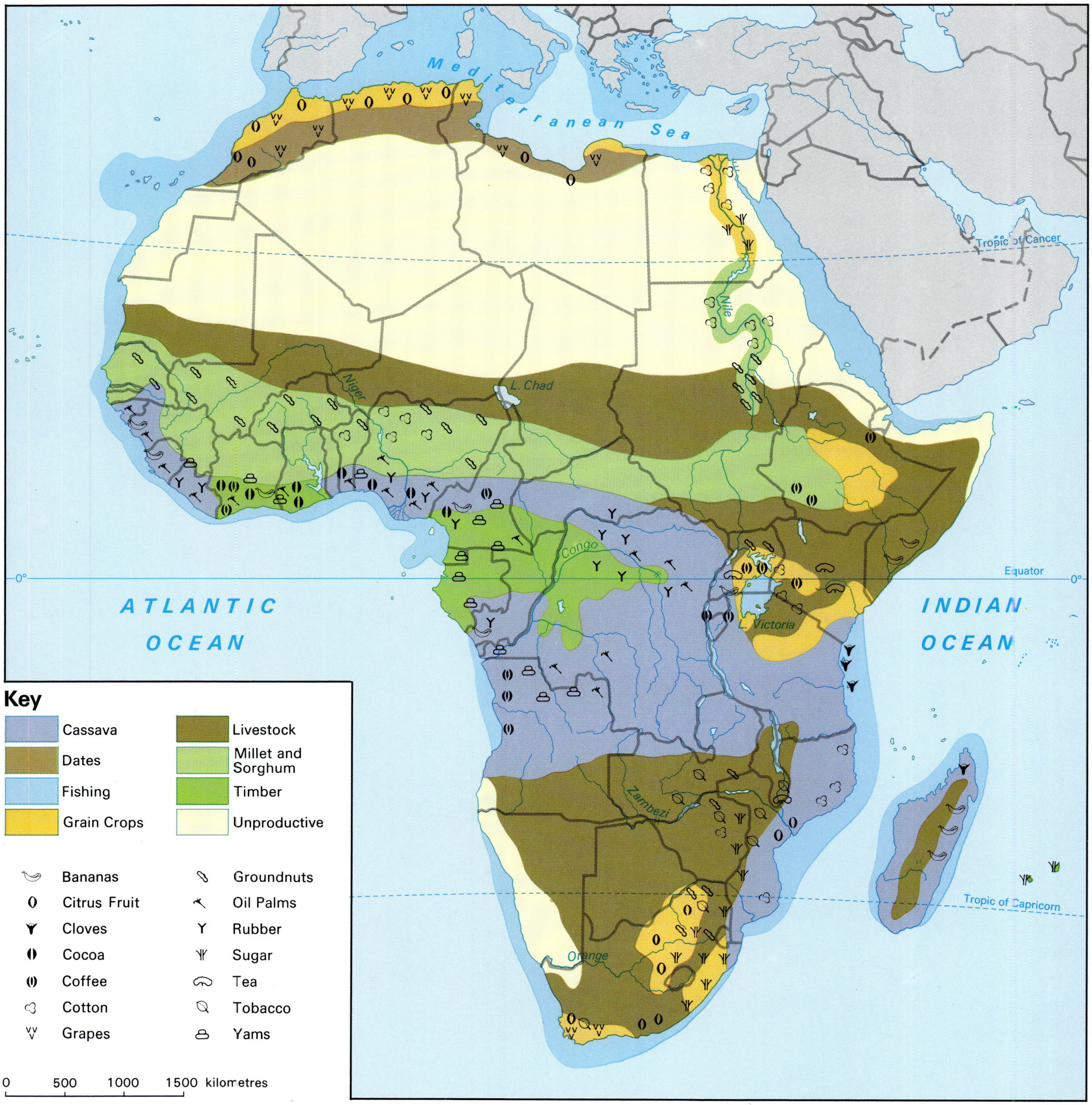

Cash Crop Production in Africa 1994

Cocoa

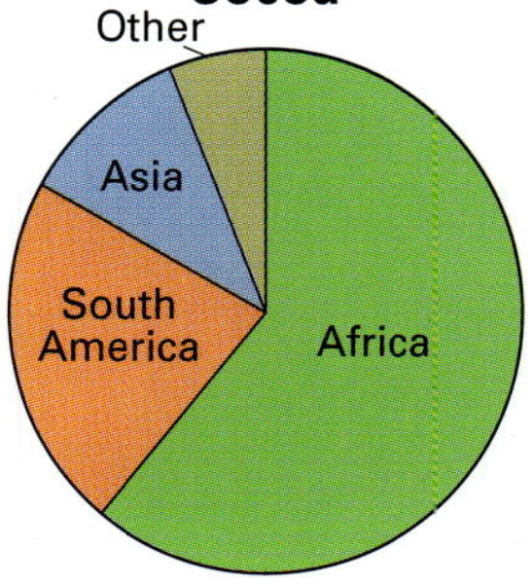

Total World Production 5.8 million tonnes

Coffee

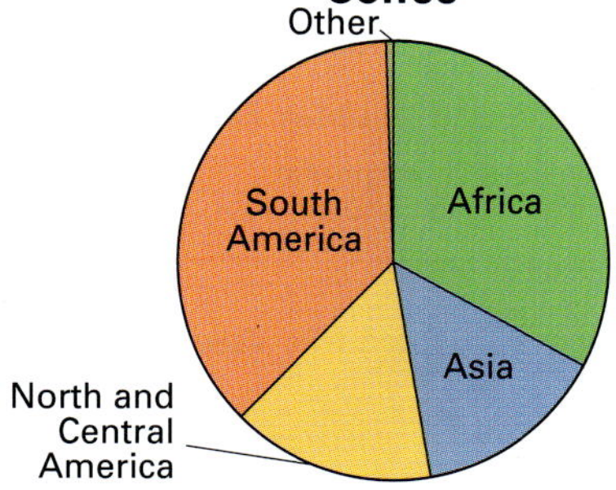

Total World Production 10.5 million tonnes

Palm Oil

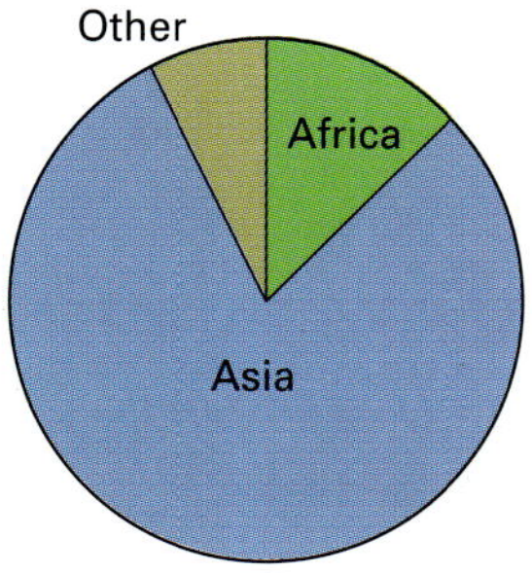

Total World Production 14.6 million tonnes

The Importance of Mineral Production in Africa 1993

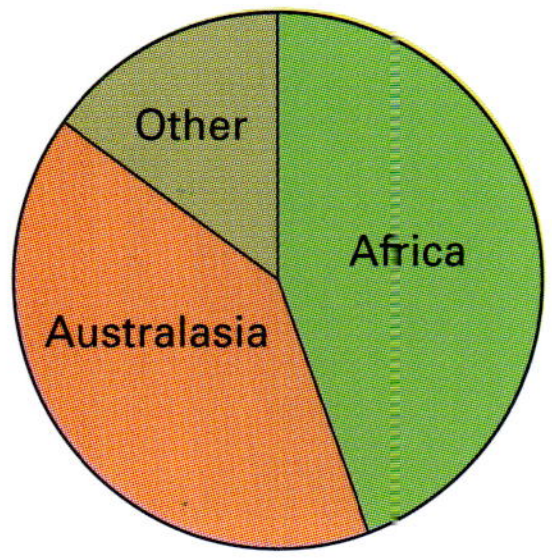

Total World Production 100 850 000 carats

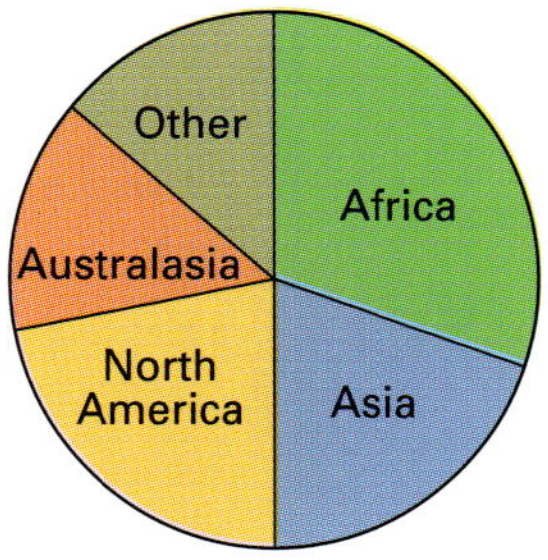

Total World Production 2 281 tonnes

Africa's share of the world's mineral wealth 1993

Mineral	*Percentage share*
Bauxite	16.3%
Chrome	34.9%
Cobalt	43.2%
Copper	7.5%
Diamonds	44.3%
Gold	30.2%
Manganese	27.6%
Uranium	21.1%

Africa Environment

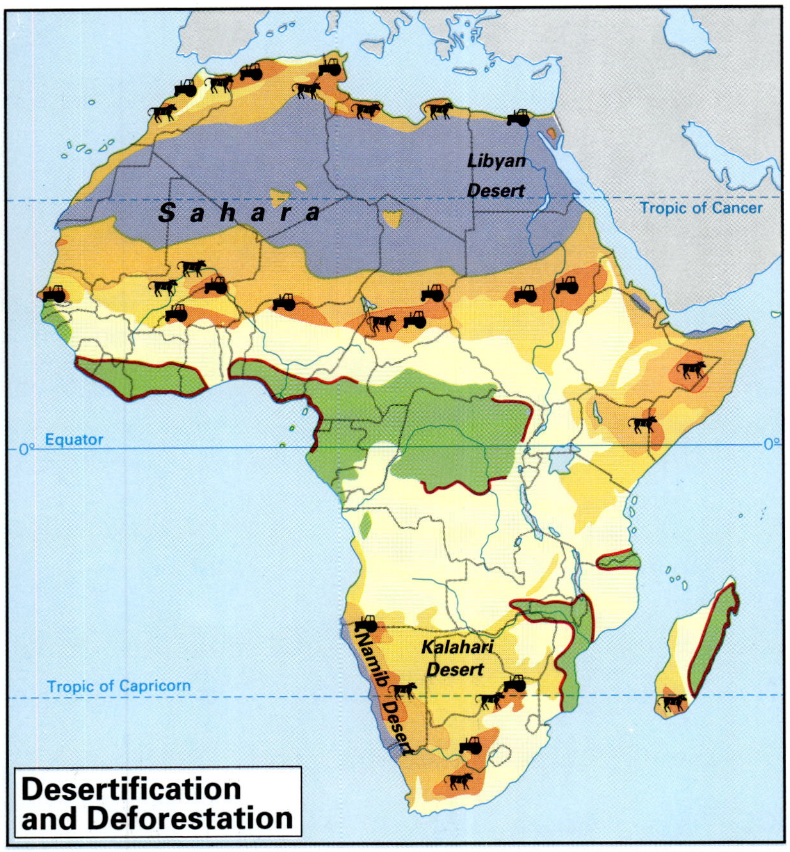

Key

Risk of Desertification

- Very High
- High
- Moderate
- Existing Desert

0 1000 2000 kilometres

Human and Animal Pressure

- Human Pressure
- Animal Pressure

Deforestation

- Tropical Forest
- Areas of Forest being cleared

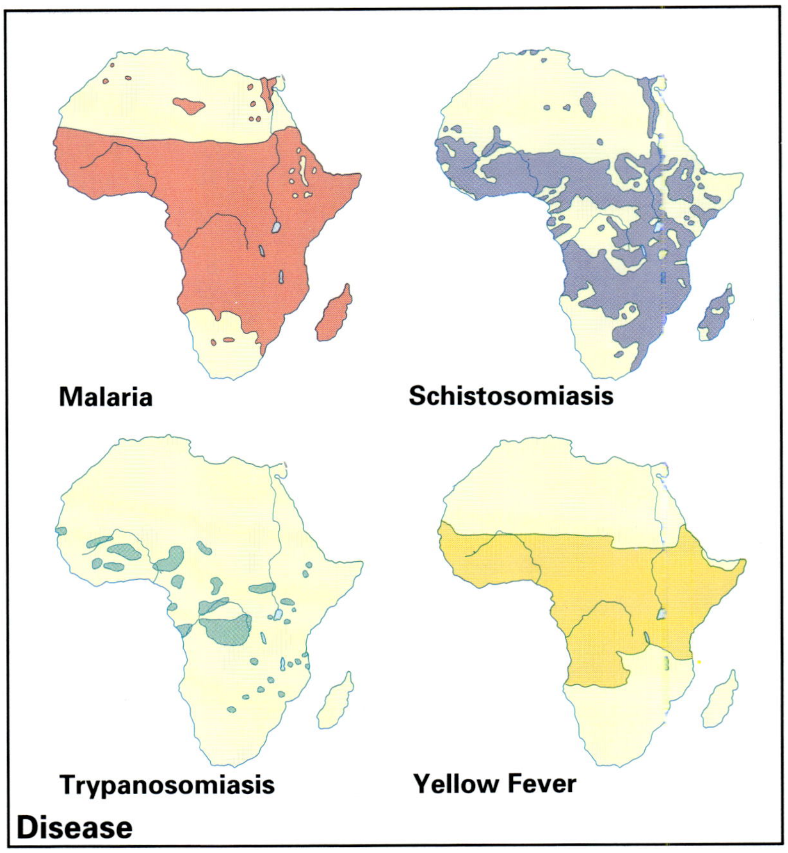

Key

Areas where disease may occur

Disease

- Malaria
- Trypanosomiasis (Sleeping Sickness)
- Schistosomiasis (Bilharzia)
- Yellow Fever

0 2000 4000 kilometres

Key

- National Park/Game Reserve

1 Kidepo	17 S. Luangwa
2 Kabalega Falls	18 West Lunga
3 Ruwenzori	19 Liuwa Plain
4 Lake Nakuru	20 Sioma Ngwezi
5 Aberdare	21 Mupa
6 Mt Kenya	22 Chobe
7 Meru	23 Hwange
8 Amboseli	24 Matusadona
9 Arusha	25 Mana Pools
10 Masai Mara	26 Zimbabwe
11 Tarangire	27 Matopos
12 Mikume	28 Gona-Re-Zhou
13 Katavi	29 Inyanga
14 Maiko	30 Lengwe
15 Kundelungu	31 Gorongosa
16 N. Luangwa	32 Bahine

- Range of Elephants
- Other Major Tourist Areas
- ★ Place of Interest

An elephant in Kruger National Park, South Africa.

Rainforest canopy walk in Ghana.

Population **Africa**

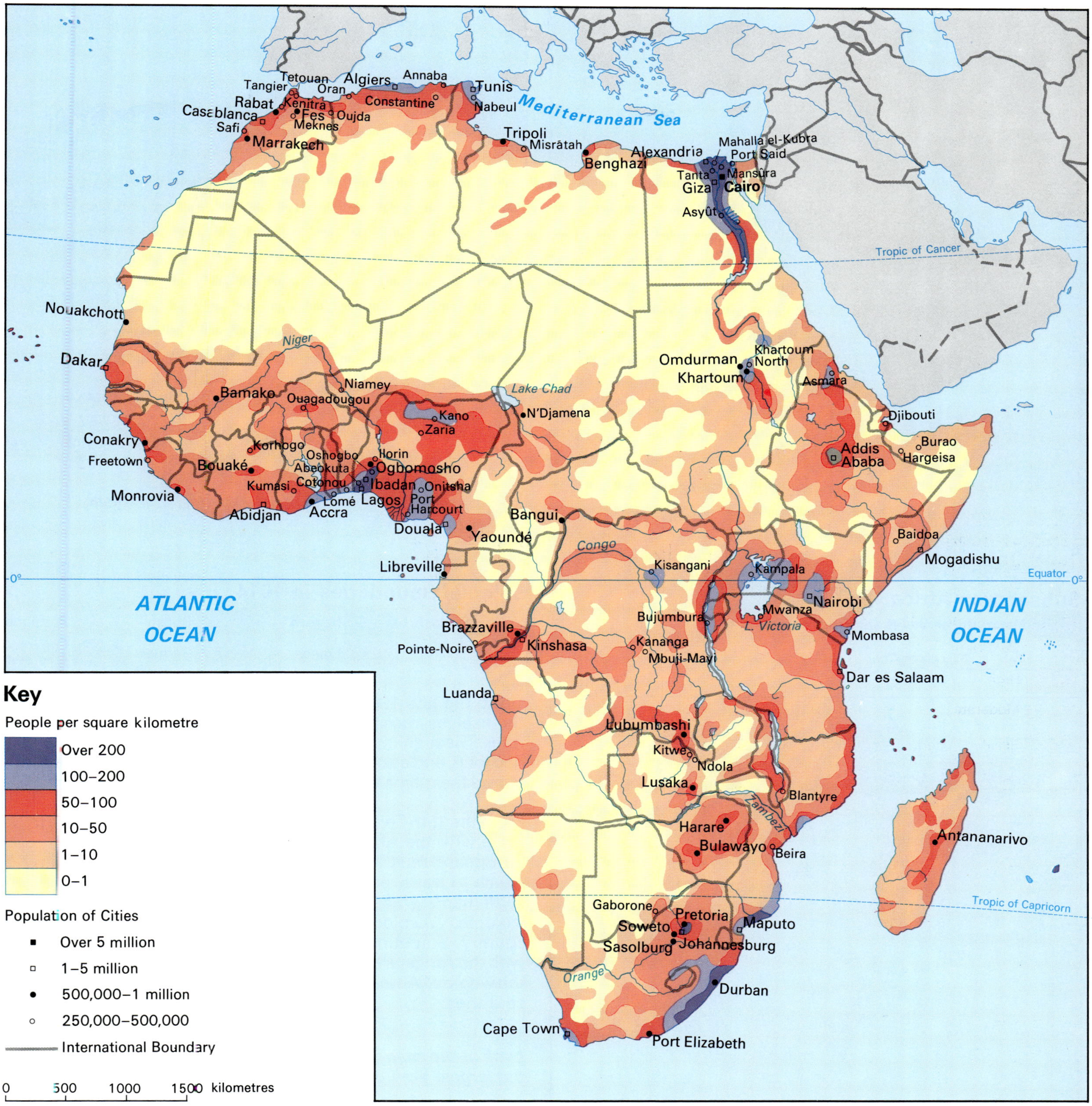

Population of African Countries 1995 (in millions)

Algeria	28.4	Djibouti	0.6	Madagascar	14.8	Seychelles	0.1
Angola	11.5	Egypt	61.9	Malawi	9.7	Sierra Leone	4.5
Benin	5.4	Equatorial Guinea	0.4	Mali	9.4	Somalia	9.3
Botswana	1.5	Eritrea	3.5	Mauritania	2.3	South Africa	43.5
Burkina Faso	10.4	Ethiopia	56.0	Mauritius	1.1	Sudan	28.1
Burundi	6.4	Gabon	1.3	Morocco	29.2	Swaziland	1.0
Cameroon	13.5	Gambia	1.1	Mozambique	17.4	Tanzania	28.5
Cape Verde	0.4	Ghana	17.5	Namibia	1.5	Togo	4.4
Central African Rep.	3.2	Guinea	6.5	Niger	9.2	Tunisia	8.9
Chad	6.4	Guinea Bissau	1.1	Nigeria	101.2	Uganda	21.3
Comoros	0.5	Kenya	28.3	Réunion	0.7	Western Sahara	0.2
Congo	2.5	Lesotho	2.1	Rwanda	7.8	Zambia	9.1
Congo (Dem. Rep.)	44.1	Liberia	3.0	São Tomé & Príncipe	0.1	Zimbabwe	11.3
Côte d'Ivoire	14.3	Libya	5.2	Senegal	8.3		

1. *Why do the following factors affect the population distribution in Africa:-*
a) Climate?
b) Altitude?
c) Urbanisation?
d) Transport network?
e) Industrial development?

2. *Cairo is the largest city in Africa with over 6,663,000 people. Which is the largest city in our country and how many people live there?*

Africa History

Subsaharan Africa 1880

Major African States and Empires around 1880

0 1000 2000 kilometres

Colonial Boundaries in 1914

Spanish	Belgian	British	Portuguese
Italian	French	German	Empires/ Free States

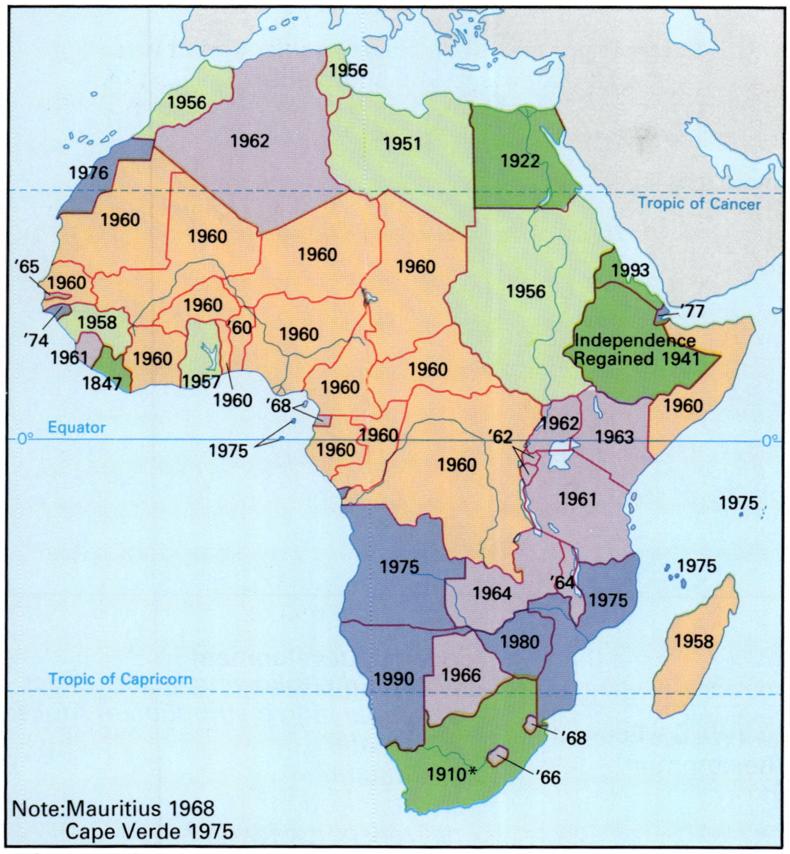

Africa Today

Date independence achieved

Before 1950	1960
1950–1959	1961–1970
	Since 1970

Up to the late 19th Century, many Africans organised themselves into **states** or **empires**, sometimes with a King as a ruler. These changed over the centuries as empires grew and declined, and as different rulers came to power. The first map shows the major states and empires that existed around 1880.

From the 15th Century Europeans had been visiting Africa to trade with the African people. As trade increased, the Europeans built settlements along the African coast from which to trade, explore and look for minerals. These settlements gradually became the bases for European '**colonies**'. A colony was an area of land ruled by a European country. Sometimes the Europeans had to fight many wars with the Africans to gain control of an area. By 1914, almost the whole of Africa had been divided between seven European countries.

Look at the map above. Which European country controlled the largest area of Africa?

Gradually the African people grew restless under European control. They wanted to set up their own governments. In each country African people began to create political parties. These political parties put pressure on the Europeans to grant them **independence**. The map on the left gives dates at which each country achieved independence.

*Although the Union of South Africa was formed in 1910 it was not until 1994 that the first non-racial democratic elections were held and a Government of National Unity was formed.

Compare the map on page 41 with the map on the left. Find Ghana. In which year did Ghana become independent?

OAU and Regional Economic Groupings **Africa**

Key

OAU – Organisation of African Unity

The dates refer to the year in which each country became a member.

0 1000 2000 kilometres

Key

KENYA EAC – East African Community

COMESA-Common Market for Eastern and Southern Africa

African members of OPEC

0 1000 2000 kilometres

Key

BADEA

ECOWAS

SADC

CEEAC

0 1000 2000 kilometres

OAU – Organisation of African Unity

This is the most important African organisation. It was formed in 1963 and aims to end colonialism and to defend the independence of its members therefore promoting unity and solidarity.

Regional Economic Groupings

Africa has a number of regional economic groupings which protect the interest of the region.

EAC – East African Community

The community was revived in 1996 to promote trade and development.

COMESA – Common Market for Eastern and Southern Africa

Previously called the Preferential Trade Area, COMESA was formed in 1993 with a view to establishing a common market by the year 2000.

OPEC – Organisation of the Petroleum Exporting Countries.

It was formed in 1960 to unify petroleum policies and stabilise the price of oil on the world market.

BADEA – Arab Bank for Economic Development in Africa

provides investment for developing projects.

ECOWAS – Economic Community of West African States.

The community was formed in 1975 to promote trade, co-operation and self-reliance in West Africa.

SADC – Southern African Development Community

was set up to unite the economic development within these countries.

CEEAC – Economic Community of Central African States

aims to create a common market with free movement of people, goods, services and capital.

Europe Physical and Political

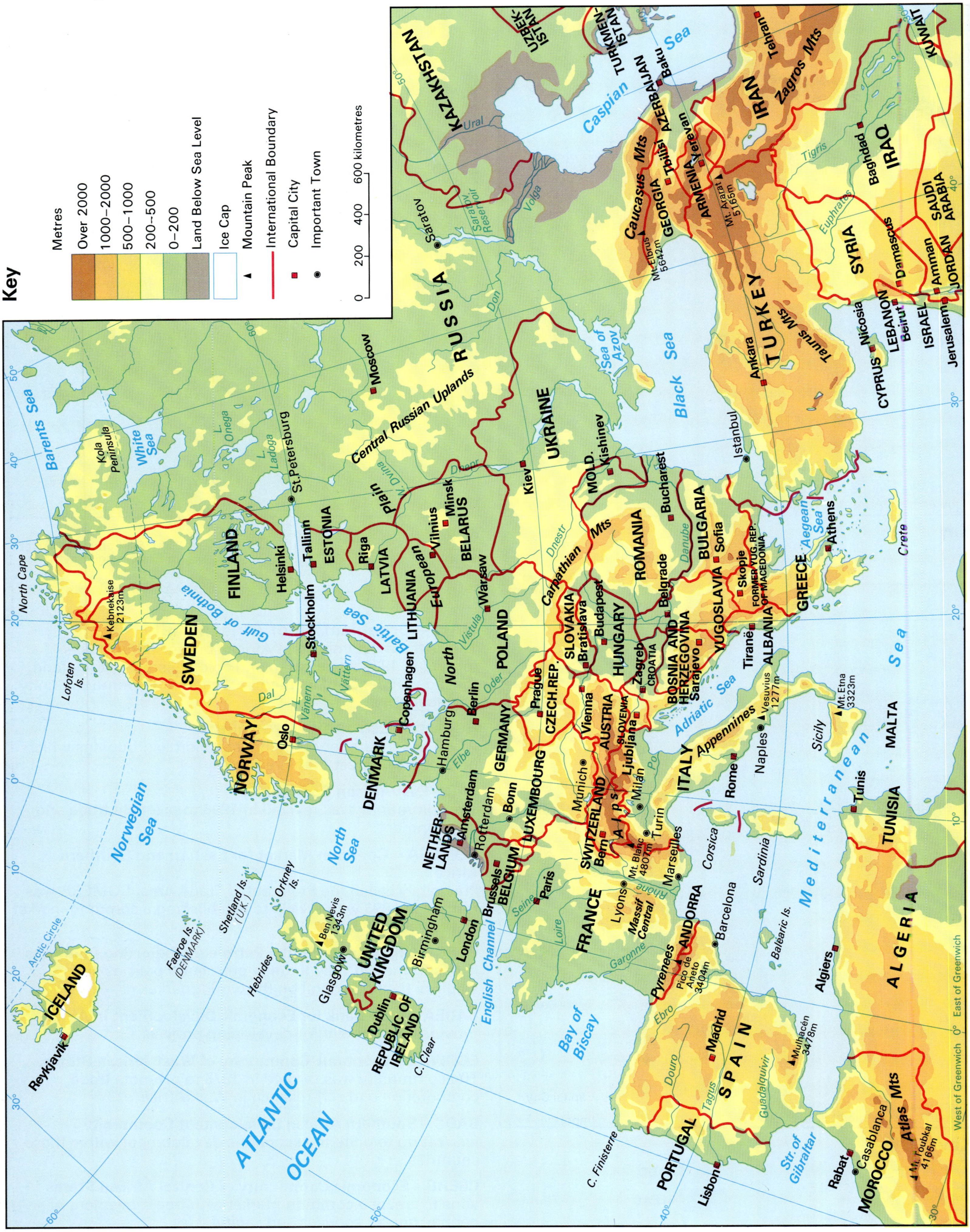

North Pole
ARCTIC OCEAN
ATLANTIC OCEAN
Norwegian Sea
Arctic Circle
Barents Sea
Novaya Zemlya
REP. OF IRELAND
UNITED KINGDOM
London
NETH.
BELGIUM
FRANCE
SWITZ.
ITALY
Rome
DENMARK
GERMANY
CZECH REP.
SLOVAKIA
AUST.
HUN.
SLOV.
CRO.
BOS. HERZ.
YUG.
ROMANIA
BULG.
ALB.
MACE.
GREECE
NORWAY
Oslo
SWEDEN
Stockholm
FINLAND
Helsinki
ESTONIA
St.Petersburg
LATVIA
LITHUANIA
POLAND
BELARUS
UKRAINE
MOLD.
Kiev
Moscow
Dnepr
Danube
Volga
Black Sea
Istanbul
Ankara
TURKEY
GEORGIA
ARMENIA
Mt Elbrus 5642m
Mt Ararat 5165m
AZERBAIJAN
Baku
Caspian Sea
Aral Sea
LEBANON
ISRAEL
SYRIA
Damascus
Amman
JORDAN
Cairo
EGYPT
Nile
Tigris
Baghdad
IRAQ
Zagros Mts.
4548m
Tehran
IRAN
KUWAIT
Kuwait
BAHRAIN
QATAR
U.A.E.
Riyadh
SAUDI ARABIA
Makkah
Red Sea
Muscat
OMAN
YEMEN
Sana'a
SUDAN
ERITREA
DJIBOUTI
ETHIOPIA
SOMALIA
Gulf of Aden
Ural Mountains
Samara
Chelyabinsk
Ob
West Siberian Plain
Yenisei
Omsk
Irtysh
Akmola
KAZAKHSTAN
L. Balkhash
RUSSIA
Central Siberian Plateau
Lena
Verkhoyansk Ra.
Yablonovyy Ra.
Irkutsk
Baykal
Altai Mts.
4506m
UZBEKISTAN
TURKMENISTAN
Ashkhabad
Tashkent
Bishkek
Almaty
KYRGYZSTAN
TAJIKISTAN
Dushanbe
Hindu Kush
Kabul
AFGHANISTAN
K2 8611m
Islamabad
PAKISTAN
Karachi
Indus
New Delhi
NEPAL
Kathmandu
Mt Everest 8848m
BHUTAN
Himalayas
Brahmaputra
Ganges
Ürümqi
MONGOLIA
Ulan Bator
Gobi Desert
CHINA
Kunlun Shan
Tibetan Plateau
Gongga Shan 7556m
Huang He
Chang Jiang
Beijing
Shenyang
Xi'an
Nanjing
Wuhan
Shanghai
Chongqing
Kunming
Guangzhou
Hong Kong
T'ai-pei
TAIWAN
Harbin
Manchurian Plain
Amur
Vladivostok
N. KOREA
Pyongyang
Seoul
S. KOREA
Yellow Sea
Sea of Japan
JAPAN
Sapporo
Tokyo
Osaka
Mt Fuji-san 3776m
Sakhalin
Sea of Okhotsk
Kamchatka Peninsula
Bering Sea
Aleutian Is.
Tropic of Cancer
PACIFIC OCEAN
Ahmadabad
Calcutta
BANGLADESH
Dhaka
INDIA
Bombay
Arabian Sea
Hyderabad
Deccan
Bangalore
Madras
Lakshadweep Is. (INDIA)
Bay of Bengal
Andaman Is. (INDIA)
SRI LANKA
Colombo
MALDIVES
BURMA
Irrawaddy
Rangoon
THAILAND
Bangkok
LAOS
Vientiane
Mekong
Hanoi
VIETNAM
CAMBODIA
Phnom Penh
Ho Chi Minh City
South China Sea
Manila
PHILIPPINES
Celebes Sea
MALAYSIA
BRUNEI
Kuala Lumpur
Singapore
Sumatra
3805m
Borneo
Sulawesi
INDONESIA
Equator
Jakarta
Java
Timor Sea
SEYCHELLES
COMOROS
INDIAN OCEAN
East of Greenwich
Tropic of Capricorn
AUSTRALIA
Key
Metres
Over 4000
2000-4000
1000-2000
500-1000
200-500
0-200
Land Below Sea Level
Ice Cap
Mountain Peak
International Boundary
Capital City
Important Town
0 500 1000 1500 2000 kilometres

North America Physical and Political

Physical and Political **South America**

Australasia Physical and Political

Physical **World**

Key

Metres

- Over 4000
- 2000 – 4000
- 1000 – 2000
- 500 – 1000
- 200 – 500
- 0 – 200
- Land below Sea Level
- Ice Cap
- ▲ Mountain Peak

0 2000 4000 kilometres

World – Continents

In this diagram the size of the continents are proportional to their actual size. The symbols represent the highest elevation on each continent and their height is proportional to the actual mountain height.

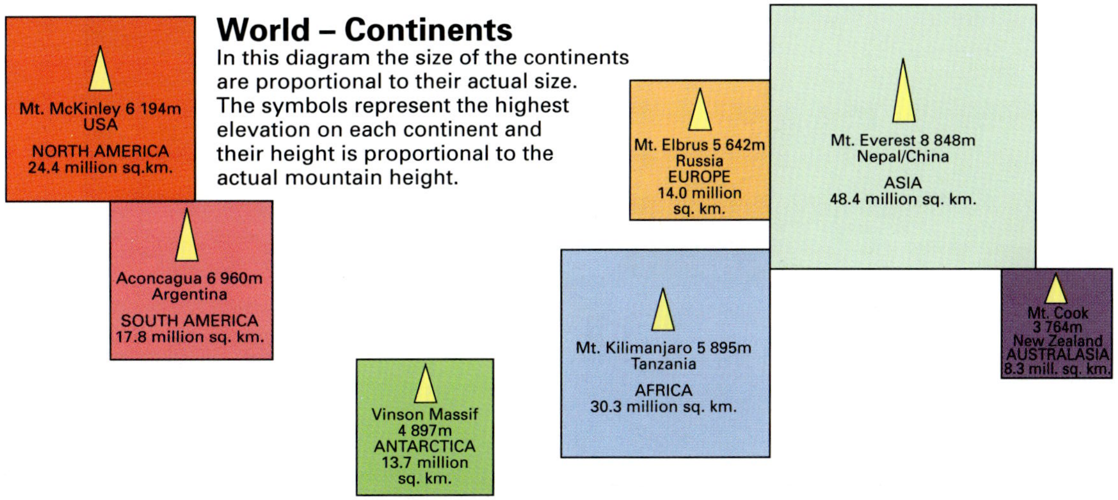

Mount Everest is the highest mountain in the world and is covered with snow throughout the year.

World Political

Key

International Boundary

Capital City

MIDDAY
12.00hrs
The clocks show local time when it is Midday on the Greenwich Meridian (0°)

0 2000 4000 kilometres

Abbreviations

ALB.	ALBANIA
ARM.	ARMENIA
AZER.	AZERBAIJAN
BELG.	BELGIUM
BOS.	BOSNIA AND HERZEGOVINA
BUR.	BURUNDI
C.A.R.	CENTRAL AFRICAN REPUBLIC
CRO.	CROATIA
DOM.REP.	DOMINICAN REPUBLIC
EQ.GU.	EQUATORIAL GUINEA
ISR.	ISRAEL
LEB.	LEBANON
LITH.	LITHUANIA
LUX.	LUXEMBOURG
MACE.	FORMER YUGOSLAV REPUBLIC OF MACEDONIA
MOLD.	MOLDOVA
NETH.	NETHERLANDS
RW.	RWANDA
SLO.	SLOVAKIA
SLOV.	SLOVENIA
SWITZ.	SWITZERLAND
U.A.E.	UNITED ARAB EMIRATES
YUG.	YUGOSLAVIA

When it is mid-day in Ghana, it is early morning in New York, on the east coast of the U.S.A.

When it is mid-day in Ghana, it is also mid-day in London, the capital of the United Kingdom.

When it is mid-day in Ghana, people in Pakistan are sitting down to an early evening meal.

When it is mid-day in Ghana, it is night-time in Sydney on the east coast of Australia.

World Climate

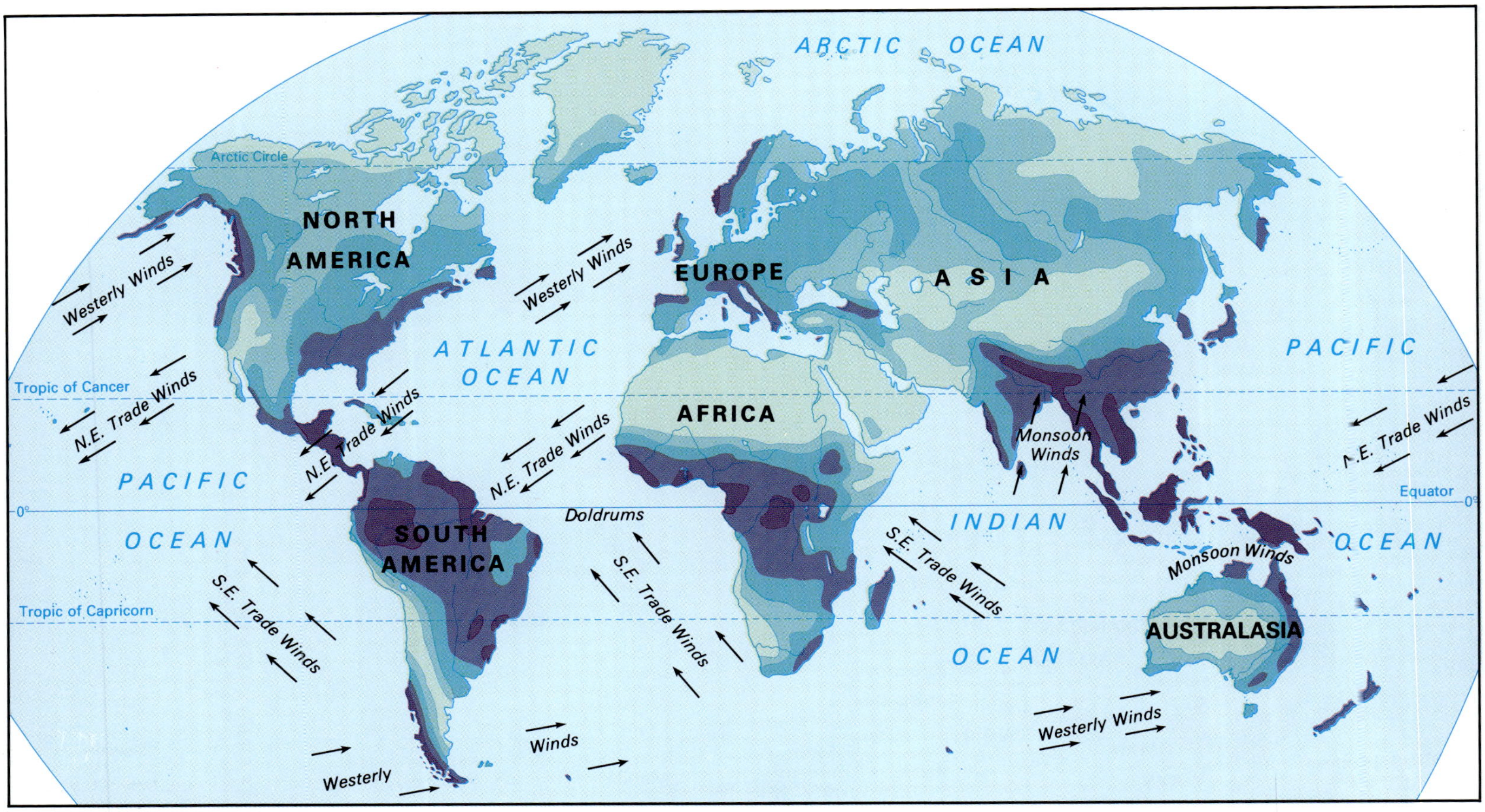

Wet and Dry Lands

Key

→ Prevailing Winds

Average Annual Rainfall

Millimetres	
Over 2000	Very Wet Lands
1000–2000	Wet Lands
500–1000	Moderately Wet Lands
250–500	Dry Lands
Less than 250	Very Dry Lands

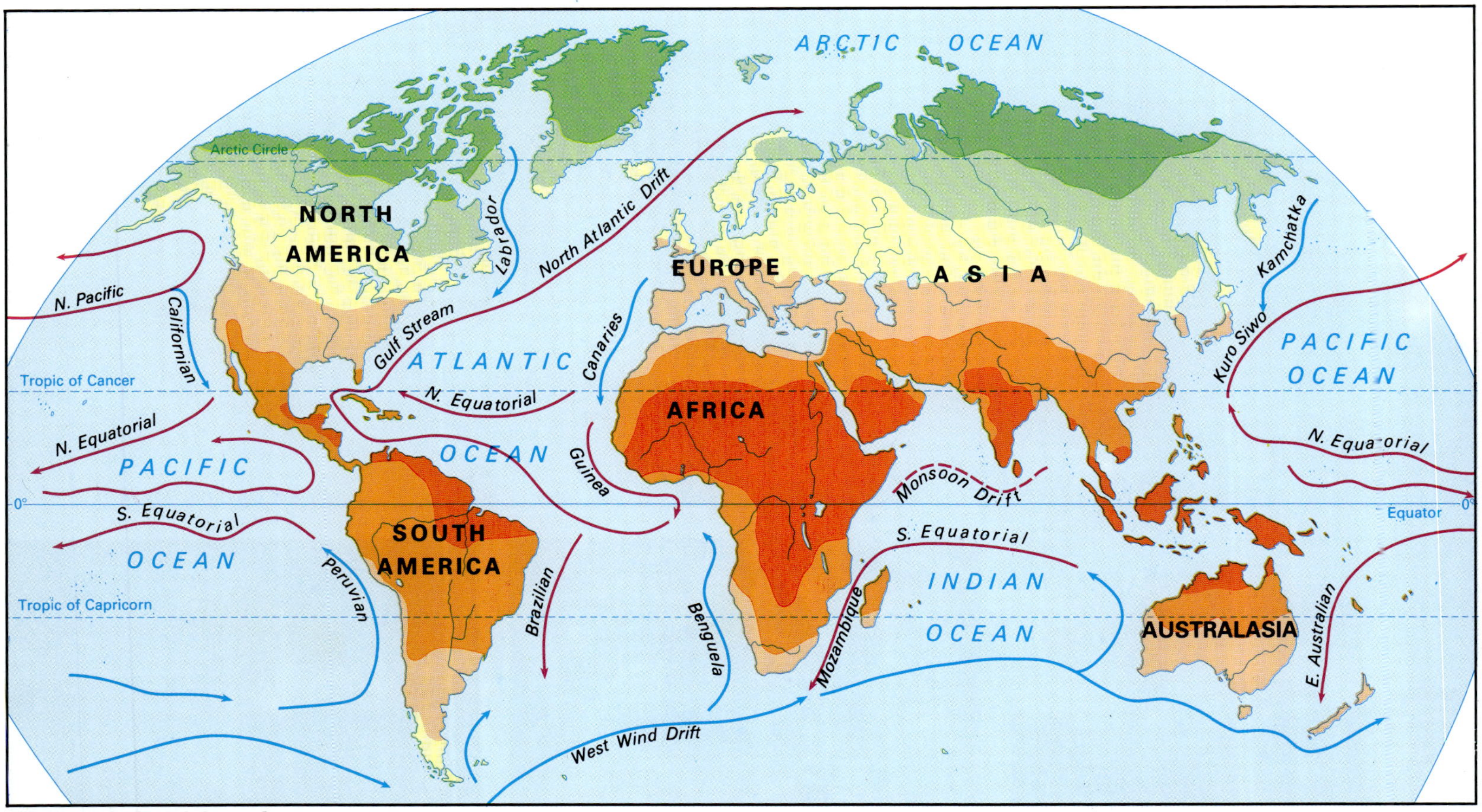

Hot and Cold Lands

Key

Warm Ocean Currents

Cold Ocean Currents

0 2000 4000 6000 kilometres

Average Annual Temperature (Sea Level)

Over 30°C	Very Hot Lands
20–30°C	Hot Lands
10–20°C	Warm Lands
0–10°C	Cool Lands
−10–0°C	Cold Lands
Less than −10°C	Very Cold Lands

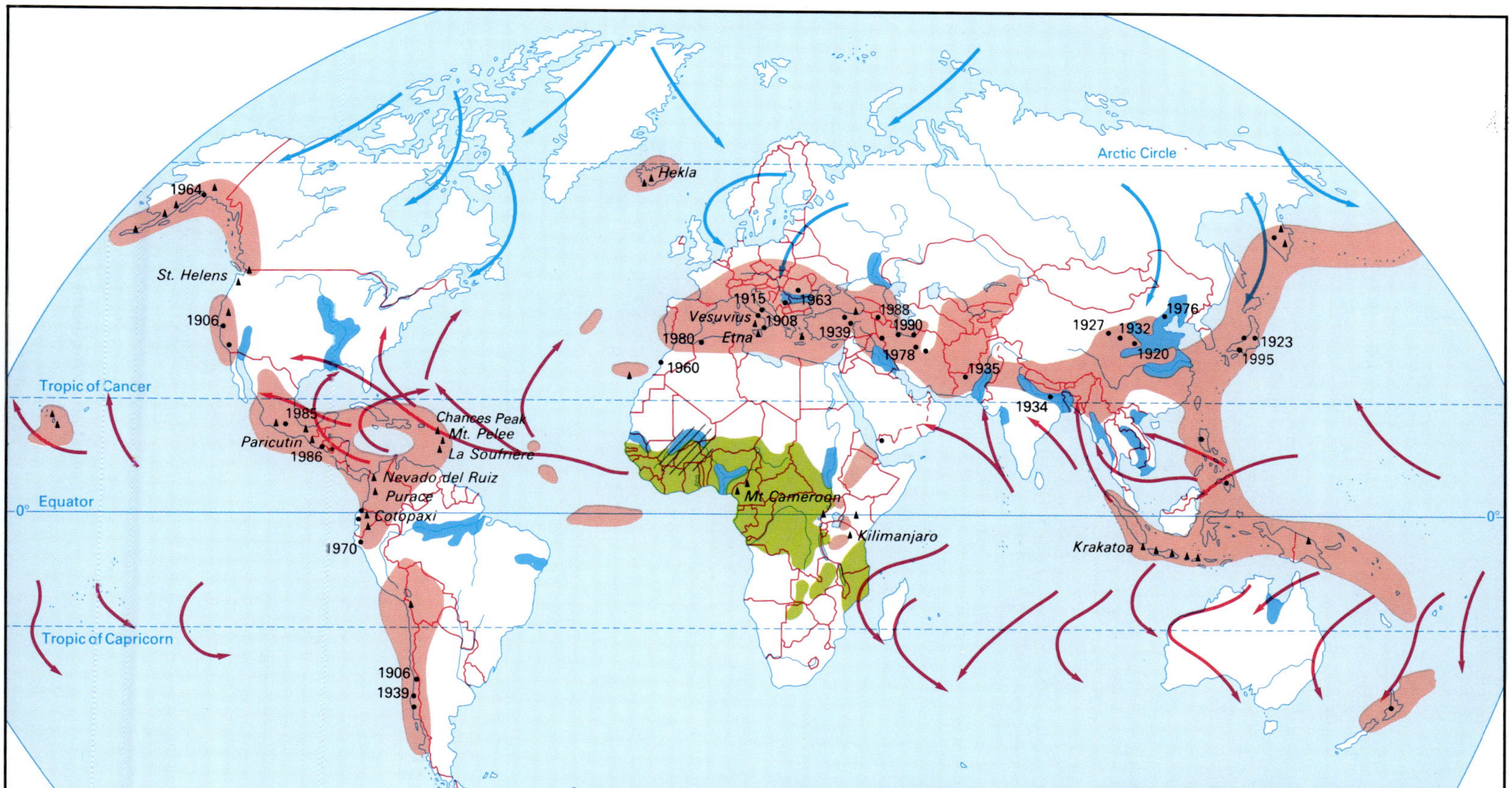

• Major Earthquake within the last 100 years

▲ Active Volcano within the last 100 years

Natural Disasters

- Main areas affected by Tsetse Flies – flies carry disease between people and animals
- Areas affected by the Simulium fly - this causes river blindness in the valley areas
- Paths of Winter Blizzards
- Paths of Tropical Storms – cyclones, hurricanes or typhoons
- Areas liable to Earthquake disturbance
- Areas liable to Flooding

0 2000 4000 6000 kilometres

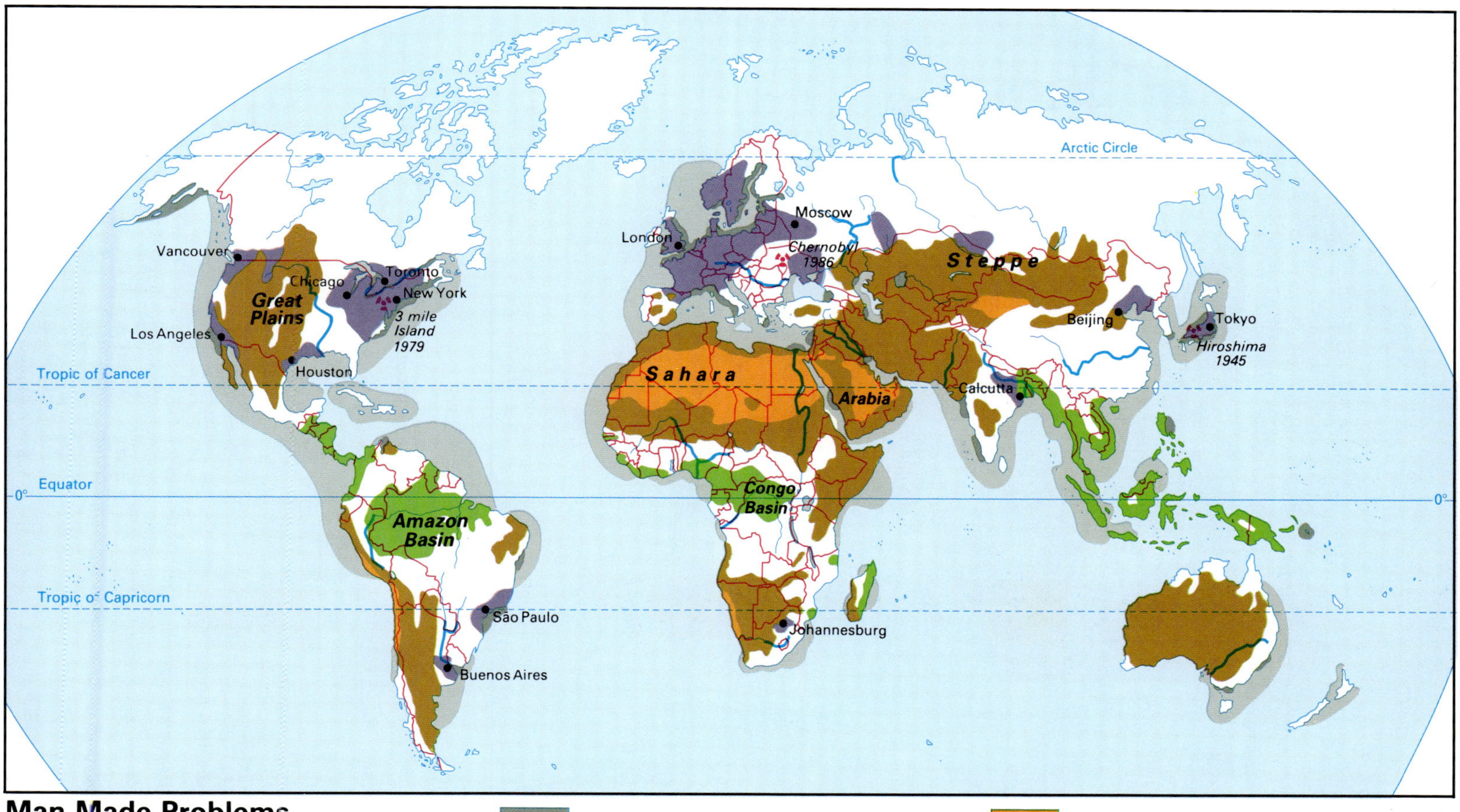

Man Made Problems

- Air pollution – acid rain and smog from major cities and industrial areas
- Radioactive Discharge
- Heavily Polluted Seas and Lakes
- Other Polluted Seas and Lakes
- River Pollution
- True Desert
- Areas threatened by Desertification
- Areas of rapid Deforestation

0 2000 4000 6000 kilometres

World Economic Activity

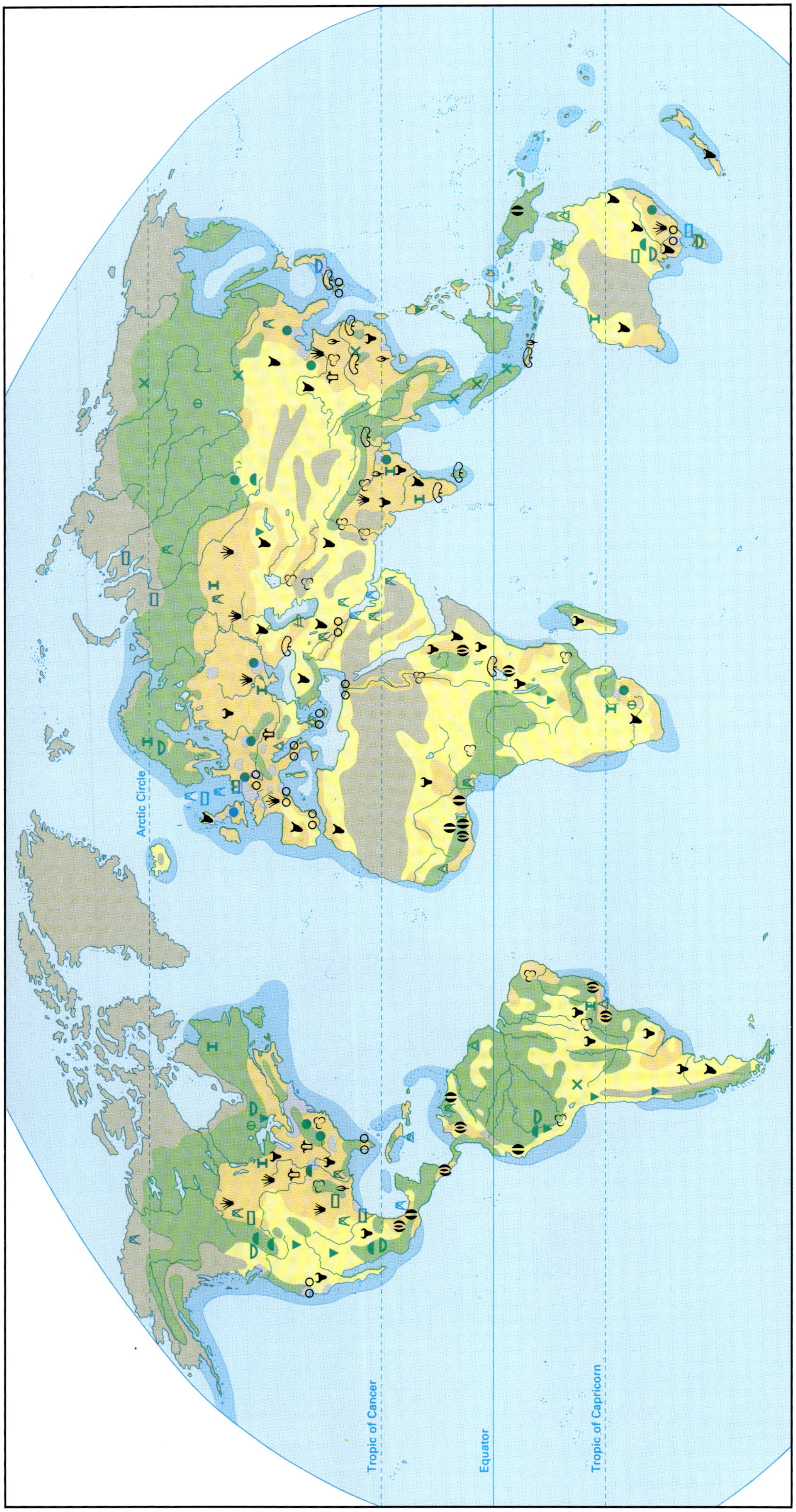

Key

- Arable Land
- Grazing Land
- Forest and Woodland
- Unproductive Land
- Major Industrial Areas
- Major Fishing Areas

0 2000 4000 kilometres

Major Crops
- Cocoa
- Coffee
- Cotton
- Fruit
- Maize
- Rice
- Tea
- Wheat

Livestock
- Cattle
- Sheep

Major Mineral and Energy Resources
- Bauxite
- Coal
- Copper
- Gas
- Gold
- Iron Ore
- Lead
- Oil
- Tin
- Zinc

Land Use
(million hectares)

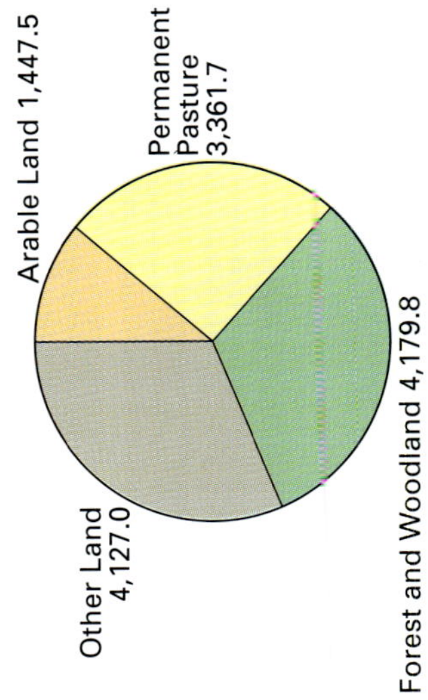

Total Land Area 13,116 million hectares

Population **World**

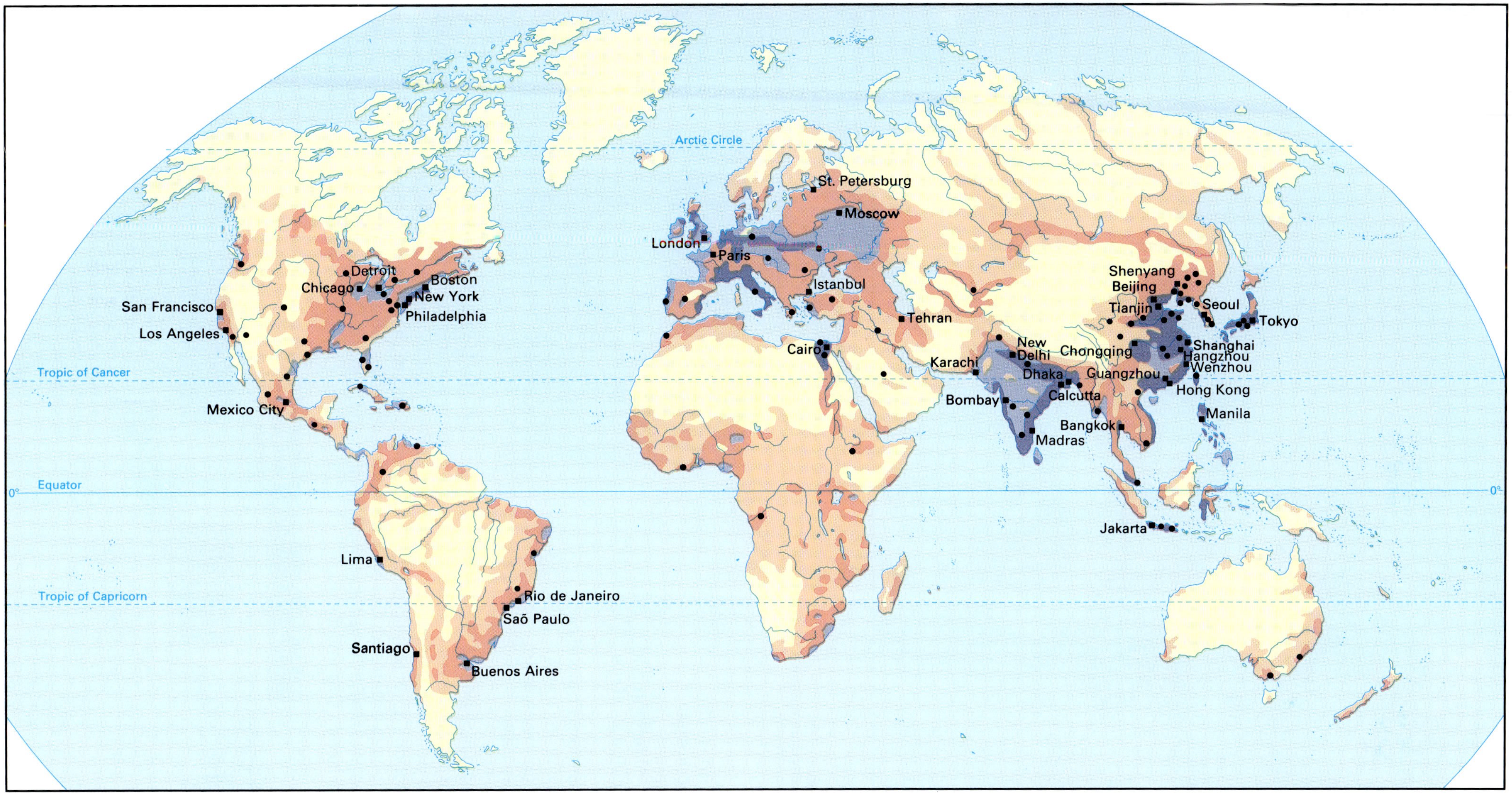

Key

Population Density
People per square kilometre

- Over 100
- 50 – 100
- 10 – 50
- 1 – 10
- 0 – 1

Population of Cities

- ■ Over 5 million
- ● 2 – 5 million

0 2000 4000 kilometres

The Distribution of Population in the World

More than half of the world's population live in Asia.

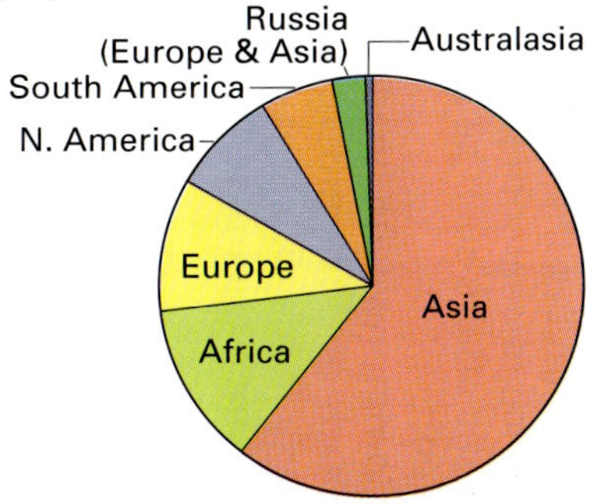

Total World Population 1995
5,702 million people.

This map shows how the population of the world is very unevenly spread. Nearly half the world's population lives in only four countries—China, India, U.S.A. and Indonesia.

The most populated country in each continent

Continent	*Country*	*Population*
Africa	Nigeria	101.2 million
Asia	China	1218.8 million
Australasia	Australia	18.0 million
Europe	Germany	81.7 million
N. America	USA	263.2 million
S. America	Brazil	157.8 million

Why is the population sparse in
a) the Sahara?
b) Greenland?

Population Distribution by Urban-Rural Areas

Less than half of the world's population lives in urban areas.

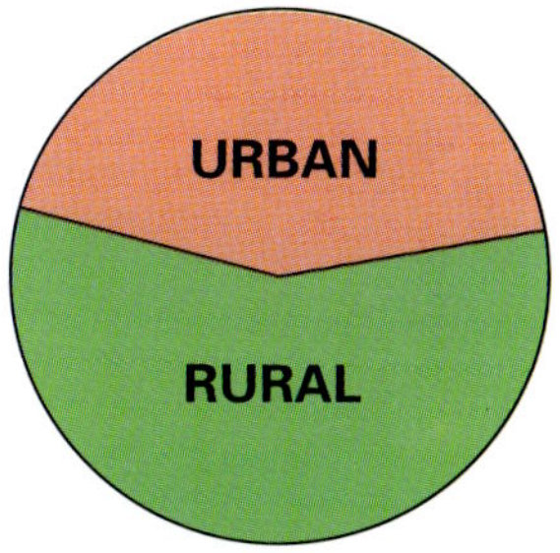

More than half of the world's population lives in rural areas.

World United Nations and the Commonwealth

Key

Members of the United Nations

Members of the United Nations and the Commonwealth

0 2000 4000 6000 kilometres

There are 185 member countries of the United Nations. Countries which are not members of the United Nations are:

Kiribati*	Switzerland	Tonga*	Vatican City
Nauru*	Taiwan	Tuvalu*	

* Pacific island countries in the Commonwealth, but not in the United Nations.

The Commonwealth is made up of 53 countries. The countries are all equal in status. There is no formal treaty or aim but the countries provide mutual assistance to each other and co-operate in all foreign and domestic affairs such as trade, education, cultural affairs and sport.
The Commonwealth headquarters are in London, England but the Heads of Government of all member countries meet regularly in the different cities within the Commonwealth. South Africa rejoined the Commonwealth in 1994.

The flag of the United Nations

After the Second World War people wanted peace and unity. On 24th October, 1945 the United Nations came into existence to promote peace and co-operation between nations. It is the largest organisation in the world and its headquarters are based in New York, USA. There are 185 member countries and they meet every year in the General Assembly to discuss their disputes and problems. The United Nations aims to help people of the world and to maintain their friendship. Below is a diagram which shows how the United Nations is organised. Several specialised agencies exist within the United Nations, each having particular responsibilities. Examples are: UNESCO (Education, Scientific and Cultural Organisation), FAO (Food and Agriculture Organisation) and WHO (World Health Organisation).

GENERAL ASSEMBLY
Consists of all members, who have one vote each. Meets each year between September and December or in emergency special session if required.

Security Council
Responsible for the maintenance of peace and security. It is composed of 15 members – 5 permanent; China, France, Russia, U.K., U.S.A. and 10 non-permanent elected for a 2 year term by the General Assembly.

Economic and Social Council
Responsible for economic, social, cultural, educational and health matters. It is composed of 54 members elected for a 3 year term by the General Assembly.

Trusteeship Council
Established to look after territories which are not fully self-governing. All the original 11 trust territories are now independent.

International Court of Justice
The principal judicial organ of the United Nations. It is composed of 15 judges, can only try cases between countries and sits in the Hague, Netherlands.

Secretariat
The chief administrative office of the United Nations. It is composed of the Secretary General and an international staff.

Seasons

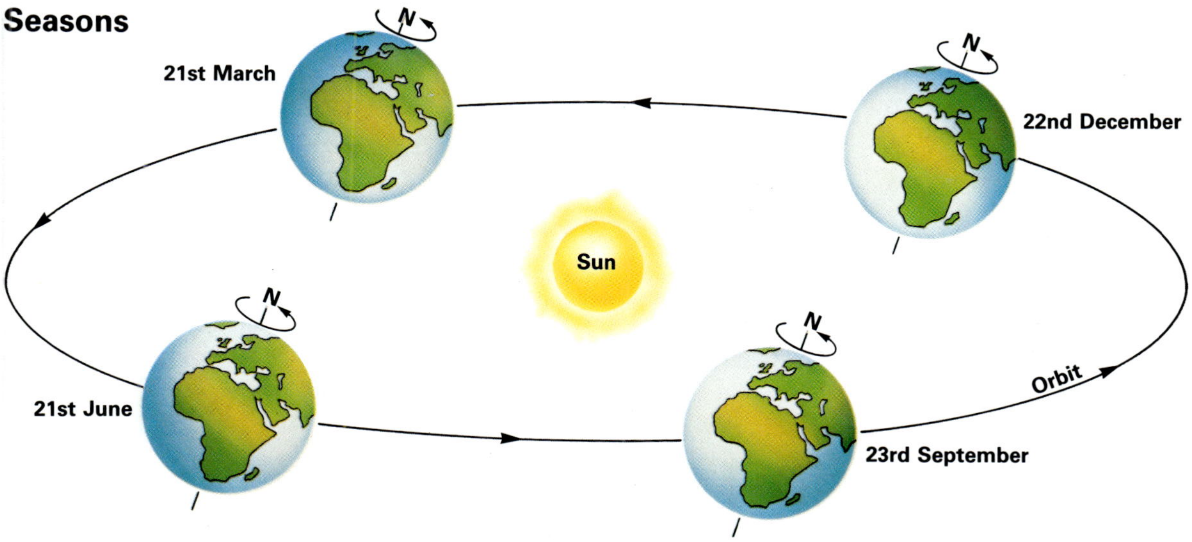

This shows the **Earth's** journey round the **Sun** in one year.

We call this journey an orbit.

It takes **365¼** days for the **Earth** to orbit the **Sun**.

As the **Earth** orbits the **Sun**, the amount of sunshine on different parts of the **Earth's** surface changes, which results in different **Seasons** – **Spring, Summer, Autumn, Winter**.

Look at the position of the **Earth** in **June.**

The northern half of the **Earth** gets more sunshine than the southern half, so northern Africa has **Summer** and southern Africa has **Winter.**

Now look at the position of the **Earth** in **December.**

The northern half of the **Earth** gets less sunshine now, so northern Africa has **Winter** and southern Africa has **Summer.**

Day and Night

The **Earth** also spins round as it orbits the **Sun.**
It takes **24** hours to spin round once.
It spins from West to East.

When **Ghana** faces away from the **Sun** it is night time.
When **Ghana** faces towards the **Sun** it is day time.

The diagram above shows the **Earth** turning.
If you could stand on the **Sun** this is how the **Earth** would look at different times during its **24** hour spin.

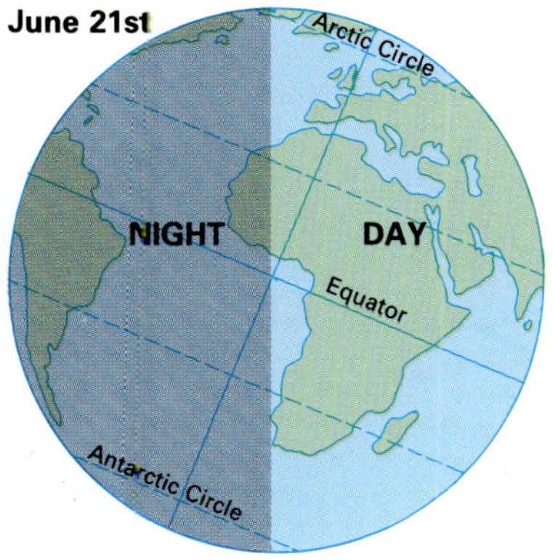

Length of Day and Night

From the **diagram** on the left you can see that in mid-June the **Arctic** has total daylight and the **Antarctic** total dark.

The opposite occurs at mid-December.
At the **Equator** the length of day and night are almost equal all the year.

On the right is a **photograph** of the **Earth** taken from **Space.**

It is day time in Africa but it is night time in countries to the East.

6 333 444 078

Index

Using the index

The index will tell you where to find places in this atlas such as countries, their capital cities, and the main towns in Ghana. For example, if you want to find Accra, the capital of Ghana, first look up the name Accra in the correct alphabetical order in the index. The entry reads:

Place	*Lat*	*Long*	*Page*
Accra, *Ghana*	5 33N	0 13W	9

It tells you in which country the place is, in this case it is Ghana. The last number tells you on which page of the atlas to find Accra. It is page 9.

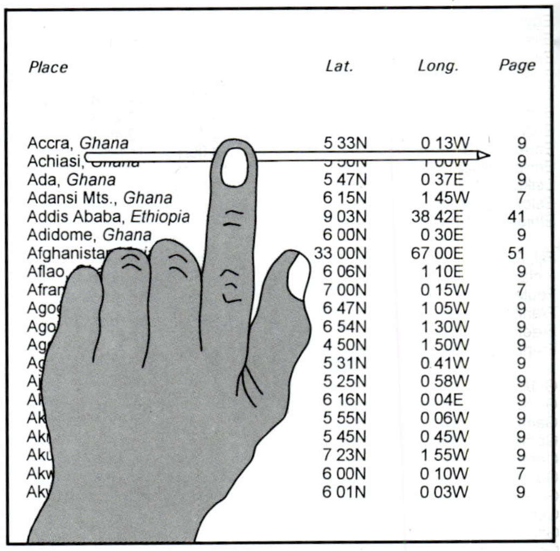

You now need to find where the place falls on the page. The index tells you by giving you the latitude and longitude. Each map in the atlas has straight lines on it. Those going from top to bottom of the page are called LONGITUDE, those from side to side are LATITUDE. The figures at the end of each line are degrees. The EQUATOR goes across the page and is at 0 degrees (0°). Latitude is measured from either North (N) of the Equator or South (S) of it. There are 90° between the Equator and the North Pole and 90° between the Equator and the South Pole. Each degree (1°) is divided into sixty minutes (60′) so Accra is 5°33′N. Longitude is measured from the 0° of GREENWICH MERIDIAN. There are 180° to the West (W) of this line and 180° to the East (E) of it. Accra lies just to the West of Greenwich Meridian at 0°13′W.

If you draw imaginary lines along the longitude and latitude figures for a place, they will cross at the place. So the index tells us that Accra is in Ghana at 5°33′N and 0° 13′W and appears on page 9 of the atlas.

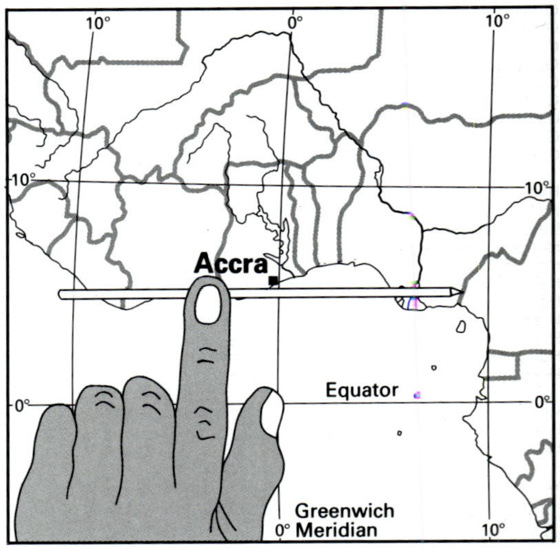

Abbreviations

C. Cape Cent. Central Comm. Commonwealth Dem. Democratic E. East G. Gulf Is. Islands L. Lake Mt(s). Mountain(s) N. North Plat. Plateau R. River
Rep. Republic S. South SADR Sahrawi Arab Democratic Republic USA United States of America W. West